THROWING Confetti

LEARN HOW TO
BECOME A VOICE
OF HOORAY
IN A HURTING WORLD

STUDY GUIDE

Throwing Confetti Study Guide

Learn How to Become a Voice of Hooray in a Hurting World

DeAnn Carpenter

ISBN: 979-8-98521-674-5

© 2024. All rights reserved. No part of this publication may be reproduced, distributed, or transmitted in any form or by any means, including photocopying, recording, or other electronic or mechanical methods, without the prior written permission of the publisher, except in the case of brief quotations embodied in critical reviews and certain other noncommercial uses permitted by copyright law.

DEDICATION

This workbook is dedicated to those wanting to make our world brighter by using what God has given you to steward. Confetti is the short-hand term for "what you have to offer." The world needs your offering. The world needs your voice and people need what is divinely yours to extend. I'd love to see confetti falling all over the globe. I have a feeling that's going to happen as we begin to practice hooray in our families, workplaces, ministries, and relationships.

Thanks to all of those who have been on the confetti journey and those of you who are about to dive in. We need more confetti cultures, more cheer, more celebrating, more hand clapping. We need more people sitting close to Jesus and offering themselves out of overflow.

Thanks to our Refuge team who daily and continually keep the confetti falling for others. I am in awe of you all of the time.

STUDY GUIDE

INTRODUCTION

YEAH, YOU'RE HERE!! I can't wait to jump into this with you. After writing the book, *Throwing Confetti: Becoming a Voice of Hooray in a Hurting World*, I've come to understand this content in even deeper ways. I'm more aware of the things that stand in the way of our applause, and I'm more convinced about the solution to our comparison problem. It is my hope that as we journey through Gods Word, sit in His presence, and reflect on what He says, we will find real solutions to our lack of celebrating because of our connection to Christ. The world needs our care more than ever and the people next to us need our confetti.

In this study guide, I want us to deal with the things that hinder our hooray, halt our voice from cheering, and learn how to hear from Holy Spirit in creative ways. I want us to encounter the living God in new ways and learn how to use our gifts in unique ways. Essentially, I want to journey through the *how* with you. How do we become more secure, more free, more of who we are meant to be? And how do we offer who we are and what we have to "throw confetti" for people? For the next thirty days we will explore these things as we engage with God, reflect, pray, listen, and practice offering.

In the back of this workbook there are blank pages for "notes," should you need extra room for journaling or reflection. Feel free to use those pages as you practice listening and leaning in with God.

BACKGROUND

I'm going to give you a little of my background in case you picked this up as a stand-alone book. As I write this, my husband Brian and I are headed into our twenty-first year of marriage. We have two incredible kids, Asher and Ruby, and a whole lot of other "kids" that we get to call our staff. My husband, Brian Carpenter, is a professional confetti thrower… basically. Together, we founded and run a non-profit called Refuge Foundation that serves to bring rest and renewal to leaders. We have a couple of Refuge locations and seventy-plus staff next to us. We've somehow created the most incredible confetti culture. Together, we set the table to bring rest and refreshment to those leading in spaces that serve other people.

We try to put an end to burnout by providing a space for meaningful relationships to be built so that connection, confession, healing, and awareness can happen. We really just make room for God to show off and create spaces for people to play, pray, and reflect. Most days, it feels like a rodeo, and we really just try to position ourselves in a way that keeps us flexible but not falling over. We get to do a lot of celebrating and hand clapping, it's barely fair. I run our women's side, "Refuge W.I.L.D." You can check it out at www.refugewild.org

It's hard work but really good work. Leading alongside our staff and serving incredible people allows me to constantly learn and re-learn lessons in confetti throwing. I've seen and experienced firsthand what a lack of applause can do in relationships. I know how competition and comparison can destroy good, and God-ordained friendships. I'd sure like to help put a stop to the criticizing, competing, and comparing that happens in us because the truth is, we need each other. We each have heavenly inspired gifts that are uniquely ours to give to others. It would be such a loss if we held back, or worse yet, if we didn't know what was ours to give.

I still believe strongly that people could use more rejoicing and less rejecting, more delighting in and less denouncing of, more bravo, more applause, and more hooray. I believe this workbook is the key to start unlocking the confetti in you in even greater ways.

Just like the book, we will start at the beginning with some origin stories in Genesis and we will wade through our beginnings too. We will search our hearts over some things, pray through a lot of things, and ask God to divinely heal and help us with the other things.

My prayer for you is that you will walk out of any previous entanglements, places where comparison has a hold on you, and grow in your understanding of your divine uniqueness. May confetti fall freely this season in the most unexpected ways *for* you and *from* you. It is most certainly a journey, but we have the most gracious guide to walk with us. God always has new ways He wants to show up and meet with us, so go ahead and get your hopes up.

LET'S BEGIN

Anytime I step into something new (like this study), I also want to acknowledge that there is usually something I need to leave behind or come out of. For instance, there's a story in John 11 that seems fitting for this analogy. It's when Jesus raises a man named Lazarus from the dead and brings him back to new life. The next thing Jesus says is that his "grave clothes" need to come off (John 11:43-44). If you are going to walk in some new things, you might need to unravel and let go of any old things that are keeping you bound. It could be an attitude, a mindset, relationship, or bad habit that's keeping you a little tied up or held back. You can always ask God if there's anything specific, but my guess is that you probably already have an idea of something that could be a hindrance.

Small shifts over time can really change the way we live. Take a kaleidoscope for example, just a small adjustment in a different direction allows for a new pattern to open up before us. I believe this study can do that. It can open up a new pattern for more generous living. Would you pause for a minute and identify a few things you'd like to personally shift or change as you begin this study? Feel free to write them down here:

_____

_____

_____

_____

_____

Let's pray, invite God into our time, and then you can pick up with "day one." Father, each person taking part in this study has a unique journey they're on, and I ask that you would meet them here on these pages and guide them each like a divine counselor. I ask that you would reveal yourself, your voice, your ideas, and your solutions. I pray you will bring comfort, peace, and hope to them as they look back and look forward. Will You awaken each heart and each mind to receive Your truth? Will You tenderly grow each of us up so that we can have lives that speak on Your behalf and reveal Your love? Help us to love You, ourselves, and others more than we think could ever be possible. Comfort us, correct us, and counsel us, speak to us Lord, we are a people in need of your continual guidance.

We look forward to all You have to say and reveal, so show us the way to take, Amen.

DAY ONE

Back To The Beginning

I can't think of a better place to start than the beginning. Let's go back to the very beginning of the Bible to Genesis, which literally means "the beginning." What we read is that in the beginning, God spoke, and something became. His sound created new spheres. His spoken words created the world. You get it, God's spoken word created something where there was nothing, and I believe that's how "having a voice of hooray" still happens in our lives. The spoken words of God's creation (that's us) are still speaking and creating things by what we are saying.

Jesus is referred to as "The Word." Then that word *became* something. "The Word became flesh…" (John 1:14). When we speak words over people, then substance is formed. Something becomes, something takes shape. If those words are life giving, then it can feel like divinely inspired pieces of confetti that fall upon or even into us. I've experienced this for myself. I've been "confettied" by God through His whisper, and I've been confettied by others through their encouragement about who I am. It's wonderful and deeply meaningful. There is another side to that coin though, and when words are not life-giving and they are spoken with ill intention towards us, those words have power too. They have the power to take something of substance from us. Words can give us security or cause insecurity, they can encourage us or take courage from us, it all depends on what we believe about them and what we believe about the person that is initiating them.

Today though, I want us to reflect on spoken words. What an idea that God chose to *speak* history into existence. He could have chosen to set the world into motion by any means necessary, and yet, God spoke and chose voice to be the catalyst for creating and initiating identity (Gen.1). Words danced around the atmosphere with the power to bring beauty into existence. It's still mind-boggling to me. Words were spoken at your very beginning too. Reflect for a minute.

1. What words were authored and offered over your life? Specifically, what role did words play for you, and how did they shape you growing up? Can you write some specific examples of how words have influenced your upbringing?

_____

_____

2. Words are no doubt powerful, a lot of them or a lack of them can greatly affect us. Wrong words issued and aimed in our direction can be detrimental to us. The right words, spoken at the right time, those words change us too, almost like someone pulled an internal confetti string. It's important to weigh the words that are spoken to us. The Bible tells us to "Guard our hearts because everything we do flows from it" (Prov. 4:23). But guard your heart too much, and it will be hard for any words to penetrate. I wonder if there are any words that you have had a hard time moving past or letting go of? Maybe ones you've spoken over someone or someone else has spoken over/about you?

_____

_____

3. Think about how you've been using words lately. Are you intentional with them, do you hold them back, do you offer them freely? What are your words doing for the people around you?

_____

_____

4. I'd like us to take a look at another book in the Bible. In James 3:1-12, James makes some really bold statements about our mouth and the power of our words. If we are going to be people who operate in a spirit of "hooray," then we have to know what to do with our words. We've got a whole study to dive in and talk about it, but for now, please, read through his words carefully and write down any reflections you have.

_____

_____

It's incredible the impact we can have on people when we choose to speak our words with intention from a place deep within us. The Bible says it's "out of the overflow of the heart that the mouth speaks" (Luke 6:45). It is from that deep well that words surface and then we bring them out into the world. Our lips move with intention and send our words to go forth with our breath.

Breath is essential for living. God brought Adam to life with breath (Genesis 2:7). The first followers of Jesus received His Holy Spirit when Jesus released His breath on them (John 20:22). In the book of Job, it says that it is God's breath that gives us understanding (Job 32:8). Breath is equated with God's Spirit in the Bible and His Spirit is still revealing things to us by His breath. Not only revealing but sometimes even initiating the words that are released from us. It's surprising, sobering even, that we have the divine ability to release words with power. Words that have power to bring life, hope, help, and even healing to another person.

PRAYER

Let's take a couple of minutes and go to God in prayer. I know we don't all have the same "practices" when it comes to prayer. We all bow our heads for different reasons; to listen, to receive, to talk, to relay information, or to ask for things we or others need. I believe God loves it all. He loves to be with us and hear from us. He also loves to speak to us about the things that we're hung up on and the things that still hurt us. God loves to commune and communicate with His kids.

Paul says in 1 Corinthians 2:10-16 that it is possible for us to hear from God and know the thoughts He thinks. Trust me, this verse is WORTH THE READ! The same God who issued the stars is still speaking to you and me. Paul tells us that we can get "the mind of God" through our connection with His Spirit. We can know what He's whispering to us or how to pray for someone by asking the Holy Spirit a question. This might be a new way to interact with God for you, though it's not necessarily traditional in most churches, it is biblical. The truth is that God wants relationship, not rulership. He wants to connect, speak, talk, and share with us. So, part of what we can incorporate in prayer includes taking time to listen to what He's saying. God seeks to soothe our anxious hearts and help direct our steps. He's a God who knows everything about everything, so let's take some time and practice listening to what He has to say to us.

This is the absolute essence of how hooray works. We partner with God to encourage a heart, whether it be our own or someone else's, not by offering our own opinions, but by getting ahold of God's opinion, and His heart. When God speaks it will always lean towards the hopeful and helpful. This is how we shift the lens for people with the words we issue and the prayers we pray. It's the "His will be done, not ours" kind of praying. When we listen with intention and expectation for His voice, we are well positioned to hear what the Triune God wants to say.

Please note, this isn't the time to be in your head or feel insecure that you "can't hear" from God. We all feel that way sometimes, and that feeling can escalate when we are about to approach God about something. Here's what we do know; we know that God loves His children, He speaks to His children, and in fact, He simply can't wait to connect with us, *His children*. If you need more convincing, please read through these Bible passages:

1. **John 3:29**
2. **John 10:27-28**

3. **Hebrews 4:12**
4. **Job 33:14-18**
5. **Jeremiah 33:3**

And then, please give this kind of prayer a chance because you can't know how powerful it is until you have tried it for yourself. Do yourself a favor and start to lean in and really listen.

In all honesty, I did not enjoy praying until I practiced listening. I felt like I was just speaking "my wants and needs" out loud into the air. But when I practiced listening to the Holy Spirit and I heard from Him, I knew there was a God actively listening and wanting to connect with me. He became a personal and relational God, someone who had answers and new thoughts for me. Someone who could really help me. God is still active and inviting us into more. Prayer is the invitation to a deeper connection with Him, the key that unlocks intimacy and mystery.

ACTIVATE

The word *activate,* according to the Cambridge dictionary, is defined as; causing something to start or to make active. At the end of most sections, we will "activate" something specific from the day that we read through. I'd like you to go back through the first five questions you answered and think about what stuck out to you? Where do you need to do some "work" when it comes to words? Do you need a new word for yourself today? Do you need to repent for something you said, or do you need to release someone in prayer, forgiving them or asking God to move on your behalf to set things right?

Some words can keep us walled in like a prison, oppressing us until we relieve ourselves from their power. God always has a better word for us, new and kind words He will offer to us if we take the time to listen. Take a couple minutes and find the relief, grace, or strength that He's offering in His presence. Feel to write down what He says here.

_____

_____

_____

_____

CLOSING

This verse from Ephesians is worth memorizing. It goes like this, "And never let ugly or hateful words come from your mouth, but instead let your words become beautiful gifts that encourage others; do this by speaking words of grace to help them" (Eph. 4:29 TPT). I'd suggest that it's not only our words but our lives that are the gifts we get to offer each other. I bet there is a "word gift" that God wants to give you today. Close your eyes for a second and ask Him what it is. Write down what you hear.

_____

_____

_____

_____

_____

DAY TWO

Words

Today we're going to look at how a few people in Genesis who interacted with words at the beginning. God gives us directions and solutions through His Word and through the words He speaks. He's been intentional about that from the start. Go ahead and read through Genesis chapter three and then write down anything that stands out when it comes to words. Extra words, a lack of words, the truth of words, the pain, and the power of them. Write down some of your observations when it comes to the role words played with the people mentioned in Genesis three.

- Adam:
- Eve:
- God:
- Serpent/ Enemy:

I hope there were some revelations or "aha moments" for you as you read through the words that were being exchanged with one another. We can learn a lot about our lives *today* based on what happened *back* then. I'd like to make a couple of observations alongside you.

Adam: Adam chose to stay silent when he knew full well what God had instructed. It's too bad because "hooray" would have really helped him. The Lord God commanded the man, "You are free to eat from any tree in the garden; but you must not eat from the tree of the knowledge of good and evil, for when you eat from it you will certainly die" (Genesis 2:16). Eve was not yet on the scene when God first spoke these words to Adam, though I'm fairly certain she would have heard them (how many times as parents do we have to give our kids the same set of instructions?). It certainly would have been nice for Adam to protect Eve and guide her back to truth, instead, he also listened as the serpent tickled their ears with an eternally devastating opportunity. We should probably pause and ask ourselves a couple of questions here.

1. There is a cost to staying silent with the people we love. We all have different reasons for why we do it. It could be a fear of something or someone. There could be demonic oppression over us (when we can't put words to why we are constrained, it feels unseen but still tangible). We might not have ever learned how or had permission to use our voices. We might still have wounds because of words

(rejection, self-doubt, fear, intimidation) so we hold back. Can you identify any reasons why you might stay silent or hold your words back from others?

_____

_____

2. Is there an area of your life or a relationship you have where God might be impressing upon you to use your voice more? (Take some time to ask Him if you're not sure about it.)

_____

_____

The Serpent: The snake used suggestive words of *comparison* with Eve to convince her to take the bite. He said aloud to her, "When she took the bite her eyes would be opened and she would be *like God*" (Gen.3:5). He handed her the thought that she could be more like someone else. The thought implies that she could be less like herself, and *more* of something. Comparing ourselves to God seems a little outlandish, but one person is all we need to make a comparison and pull out the measuring line. Who do you compare yourself with and what effects does it have on you?

3. I think it's important to identify the places where we can get tripped up. Sometimes it's a weakness in us that has us looking for more, and sometimes it's a deliberate attack from our adversary making us feel like we have to be *more*. The point is that there are plenty of things in our lives to distract and discourage us from all that God wants to give us. The Serpent used persuasion, deception, comparison, and doubt to make his case with our first two parents and I think our adversary still does that today. Has the enemy been whispering to you, tempting you, persuading you, or twisting something that God has said? It's certainly easy to see in culture, different ways the enemy undermines and distorts God's word, but how about for you personally? Can you identify doubts, comparisons, or places of temptation that could set you back this season? Please explain.

_____

_____

Eve: Eve didn't hold onto God's word. She was persuaded by a slithering wordsmith and seduced by the snake as he suggested there was *more* for her. It makes me wonder, in a world that is always offering something to us, is it hard to stay grounded in who you are? What areas of your life would you like to be more content in?

4. Next, I want to ask you where you go to get your "truth" when the enemy is flipping the script on you. Really think about this one. Absolutely we want to go to God's word and seek Him for the answers because, The One who is The Truth will have Truth to give us, but there are so many options for us. What are your tendencies when you're in need? What do *you* do and where do *you* go?

_____

_____

_____

_____

5. God gives us His word as a standard for Truth. We don't have to to wonder about what God thinks or what God has said about most things… However, even in the Church the word "truth" is getting more and more outdated. If we don't like what God says, it's easy to dismiss it. If His word doesn't "fit" us or our lifestyle, it's easy to throw it out. It makes me think that even though numerous decades have gone by, the enemy is still using the same trickery today with one common phrase; "Did God *really* say?" (Genesis 3:1). If we don't know what God has said, then we can be easily fooled. It's a good strategy for our adversary I guess, because why change what is easily working with God's kids?

_____

_____

_____

_____

Friends, this is not a season to simply "wonder what God says" about things. Let's dig in and do the work to find out. Let's submit ourselves to prayer, let's read up on His word, let's do some study, and engage in meaningful conversations about the topics we are tiptoeing around because we can find ourselves in Adam and Eve's position really fast. That's where our wondering turns into wandering simply by staying quiet and chewing on the wrong thing. Is there something that God has said (either in scripture or a personal word to you) that you are having a hard time with? What is it and what is God saying about it?

PRAYER

I'd like to close this section by inviting God to sit with us. Let hooray come for you. Let God-ordained words land timely in your heart to help heal, soothe, and encourage you, then watch for the confetti to fall. When we are full, we offer from a place of fullness, or at least "fuller-ness." When we become the recipients of Heaven's confetti, then we shine just a little brighter and have a more in our pockets to offer.

I want to circle back to comparison and invite you to sit with the Holy Spirit and ask some specific questions. Questions like; how am I struggling with comparison in my life? Who am I comparing myself with? What is the cause of my comparison? How does God see me? You might have other wonderings in mind that you'd like to have Him address from the observations you just made, please make your hope known. Give Him some time to speak and encourage you in His own way.

I'd love to start the prayer by asking you to be open and receptive to His words! Lord, we are asking for You to speak and reveal Your truth to our problems, wonderings, and feelings. We call our spirits to attention, to hear from You as You offer hope and healing. Show us things from Your perspective. Be gracious with us as You unveil what's hidden and align us with Your truth. We trust You and love You, Lord….

Take a couple of minutes and write down what comes up in your heart/mind. He speaks, He cares, and He is engaged with all that's happening in your life. I can give you plenty of Bible verses for that, but friend let me just tell you that I KNOW—I KNOW—I KNOW He has something to say to you personally. Let Him be as creative as He wants to be. You might remember a song, hear a verse, feel an impression, or have a strange assurance that all will be well. You might get a text from a friend, or you could see a picture in your mind about something specific God chooses to illuminate for you. I don't know how He will choose to show up, but I do know that if you allow Him the opportunity, then He certainly will.

This is how we start to partner with Hooray. We get quiet and we get close to the One who has all kinds of words to say to us. We catch the whisper and allow those words to fall like seeds in the fertile soil of our hearts. Write down what you'd like God to address and write down His response.

DAY THREE

Eve

We have so much to still learn from our first mother, Eve. Wow, I have a lot of compassion for her, nobody wants her legacy. Who would want to tell the story to generations behind you that yes, it was *me* who reached out and took the bite of the forbidden tree and pushed humanity outside the garden? I did what I was told not to do and then I urged my husband to do the same. I listened to the liar, I wanted more, and then I hid from my Maker.

And ever since Eve's bite, we have all hungered and wanted for more. We could tread in these waters from Genesis three for the rest of this study guide, but it would be hard to get to confetti throwing if we did that. Let's see what we can learn by looking at the conversation the Serpent used to trip up Heaven's first daughter. Please go back and review the words from Genesis 3:1-4.

   1. What words did the Serpent use with Eve to convince her and what was her response?

_____

_____

_____

The Serpent doesn't waste much time, by verse five he calls Eve to the measuring line. Measuring lines are dangerous because we will never be able to measure fairly. We don't have the same starting point. Our upbringings, backgrounds, and lens on the world do not allow us to measure accurately. That means that how we measure "up" or what we measure ourselves against is like measuring a dog against a cat, or a zebra against a giraffe. We are made with different stripes on purpose, and we will miss the beauty of our uniqueness when we try to calculate if we "add up" based on another.

Measuring makes us forfeit the divine and unique portion of ourselves, and people need that portion of ourselves. It's why the enemy comes the way he comes, so that you hold back, shrink, displace, puff up, become proud, etc. It's a terrible trick to be determining our worth, "for better or worse" by the attributes of others or by the things they have.

Where are you vulnerable to comparison in your life?

2. Eve wanted "more," and it killed her original design. Each of us at some point will struggle with "wanting more" or wanting to "be more" like something or someone. Is comparison difficult for you? Do you struggle with wanting or needing to be more?

Friend, if you're feeling "less than," you are not alone. Eve had it all and still reached out because she wanted more, she wanted to be more. I believe that when we acknowledge it, we can rightly deal with it. Insecurity is just security in the wrong place. So, when feelings surface to tell you that you're "not enough" or you "don't have what it takes," it's good information that lets you know you need to re-direct where and what you are placing your security in. How are you securing yourself in this season of life? What makes you stay grounded?

PRAYER

I want to end the day by taking some time to sit with God. I believe He has some things He wants to say to you that could really change how you see yourself. When we feel restless, insecure, or inadequate, I think the most stabilizing thing we can do is get connected to our Maker. Abide in Him and let Him speak Identity over you. If you're feel good and solid within yourself, I can assure you that He still has something He wants to say to you.

Would you ask God some key questions. First, where/what are you finding your security in? Second, what does God want to say to you? Last, I believe God has a name He wants to call you. Jesus secures one of his disciples in Mathew 16:18 by changing his name. Simon (meaning "to hear") is called Peter (meaning "the rock"), and I think God still secures, settles, and speaks to us by extending names over us. Just give it a try and write down what you hear.

DAY FOUR

We are going to continue today by observing Eve.

1. Please read Genesis 3:6 and then read 1 John 2:16. Write down what you are most susceptible to in this season of your life.

___

___

2. Eve was tempted with specific things, none of which we have a pass on. The world is loud, our flesh is hungry, and we would be wise to know the things that trigger us. How can you protect your spiritual health this season?

___

___

3. Before Eve saw and took, she was tempted by what she heard. Our actions follow what our hearts believe. I'm wondering what you've been hearing lately. Take a minute to get quiet and ask God if there are any lies you need to confront. Is there a word on repeat you can't get over? What kind of "self-talk" is your mind feeding you? Let's take some inventory of what's playing in our ears and on our hearts right now and examine how it's making us feel. Write down what surfaces.

___

___

4. We know the enemy came with twisted words to tempt Eve. He revised God's words of instruction, he cast doubt so that Eve would question God's goodness towards them, he used the measuring stick as bait, and then Eve gobbled up all that the Serpent was serving to her.

It all feels like it happened so fast. Did she have time to filter what the Serpent was saying? Was she so hungry she couldn't think straight? Did she even consider talking things over with Adam? It seems as though Eve's voice went silent too. The more the enemy spoke, the more he offered, the more Eve considered. Maybe she stood there a little too long. Is there a "tree" you're eating from right now that isn't producing good fruit in your life? This could be listening to man's opinion instead of God's instruction. This could have to do with a friend's influence, fantasies, complacency, shopping, drinking, etc. We all have different "trees" or tendencies, places we go to when, just like Eve, we *want* more, or we want to *be* more. The reason Jesus tells us to abide in His vine (John 15) is because there are so many other places for us to abide in. Not all places of abiding will produce what's good or keep us connected to Christ. Write down the places that you like to abide and consider the fruit it produces in your life. We don't want to stay too long in places that might feed us for a moment but leave us empty in the long run.

_____

_____

_____

Eve offered her bite. AGH! This scene feels like Eve is silently saying a thousand words to Adam. Almost like she's inaudibly asking, "Will you come with me, or am I in this alone?"

I don't know a gentle way to say what I'm about to write so please hear it in love…we've got to own our stuff; we just have to. It's part of growing up. We need to own our mistakes, own up to our shortcomings, our humanity, our flesh, and our appetites. We are not perfect people, we will make so many mistakes in our lifetime, but we don't need to invite people to join us when we know we're on the wrong side of something and then blame them for our "bite." It makes me think of a story…

When I was in high school, I desperately wanted to drive a car. I was still a year out from getting my license, but opportunity came knocking. My parents were out one night, and I had a friend over. I didn't need to converse with a snake because I knew how to make my own trouble. I mentioned to my friend that this would be a great time to test drive my dad's truck and take it to the store. I wiggled the keys in front of her and she grabbed her coat and jumped in the front seat beside me.

I had plenty of opportunities before that night to drive my dad's truck, but then the blame would have only been on me if I would have gotten caught. There is something reassuring about bringing people with us when we know we are about to wade into dark waters.

I guess the question I'm asking here is this; is there something you are being tempted with right now that you know could be harmful to you or someone else? I'm just asking because if we are going to be true voices of hooray for people, healthy, and healed confetti throwers, then we need to become self-aware over the things our heart's desire. We need to reflect and consider. What do I need? How am I getting what we need? Is it a healthy way to get my needs met? Because friend, we could get into real trouble, or at least experience some set backs if we don't take inventory of our hearts.

_____

_____

_____

I think this kind of maturity, to watch over and guard our hearts, can take a long time. But journaling and taking intentional time to explore our own hearts will help move us forward. It didn't seem like Eve took much time to count the cost of her taking. She saw, she wanted, she took, she offered, and then she lost so very much. I want to learn from those before me and do better. I want to have people beside me who voice caution and speak truth before I make a mess of something. And I want to be that voice for others too.

PRAYER

We will close this section with prayer and ask God to specifically show us something concerning our own hearts. The last question was a reflection about our needs and the things we desire. Sometimes, we know those desires, we know why we desire them, and we know where it's coming from. For instance, you might desire to feel seen and wanted. Maybe that desire is coming from being single and wanting somebody to pursue you. That would be an honest and healthy desire. However, maybe it's deeper than that, maybe God wants to reveal something to you and show you the "deeper" of where that desire is coming from. I'm not just talking to the single person. I'm saying that for all of us, whatever our "desire" is in this season, let's let God speak to it. Let's let Him reveal something to us about it. Let's not assume we know what it is and why it's landed in our hearts. Let's let God speak to us, let's let Him reveal a solution, speak a promise, or bring us some comfort. Let's let God be hooray for our hearts and open ourselves up for confetti in whatever way He chooses to fashion it for us.

I'd suggest you play some soft music, maybe something instrumental with no words so that you can just listen for God to say or show you something. Then, present yourself with hands open and your heart surrendered. Close your eyes and listen. Maybe a memory will surface, or you will feel a specific feeling around a need you have. Ask God to show you more, engage with Him so He can keep going with you wherever this takes you.

I used to just be content with the first thing God would show me. I was just thankful to hear from Him, I didn't realize that what He was saying or illuminating to me was an invitation to more. More of His presence, more of His voice, just more closeness and engagement.

Prayer with God is like driving down a two-way street, it's not a "one-way" road. He's not giving us information or orders to just send us on our way. God wants to bring us close so He can speak and sit with us awhile. He wants us to engage Him in our processing, healing, hurting, wondering, and celebrating. Get someplace quiet and take the next ten minutes to engage with God. Let this time be His time. Don't make any prayer requests (you'll have plenty of time for that throughout your day) just ask the Lord to speak to you today concerning *your* needs. What are they, where are they are originating from, and does He want to meet them for you? Ask what you'd like and then let the music play. Feel free to write it down here.

DAY FIVE

Connection, Covering, & Leaving a Mark

I'm still thinking about Eve and how bad it feels when we blow it. She tries to find comfort by covering herself, if that isn't a pause for reflection then I don't know what is. In fact, she and Adam hide the most intimate parts of themselves, no longer feeling free to be fully known in each other's presence.

Hiding ourselves from one another and from God doesn't lead us toward healing. Good thing God knows that. He comes for the cowering couple and starts the conversation by asking, "Where are you?" (Gen. 3:9).

1. Why don't we stop for a second and assess how we are doing with God in this season of our lives? Like all relationships in our life, this one ebbs and flows too. Good relationships take time and intention from us. If God would ask you the same question, "Where are you at?" what would your response be? Where are you in proximity to Him? Where are you at in your connection to Him? When it comes to honesty and trust, what kind of relationship do you have with Him? Are you hiding intimate parts of yourself/your dreams, etc.?

   _____

   _____

2. I wonder what God thought of Eve's new wardrobe. The Bible says that she sewed some fig leaves together to make a cover for herself (Gen. 3:7). I find that so inventive. In fact, we are still inventing all kinds of interesting ways to manufacture our own personal coverings. For Eve, it happened when she realized she was naked and exposed. Let's make it personal for a minute. Reflect about what it is that makes you feel most vulnerable or exposed? What kind of ways do you cover and protect yourself?

   _____

   _____

I'm wondering how long it took for Eve to recover after all that ensued after her bite. It takes me some time to move forward after I've blown it. Shame can really mark a person. It will keep us stuck, quiet, and hidden. And if we stay quiet and hidden, it will be really hard to be hooray for people.

I'm so thankful God had a remedy in mind for our first parents, for us here and now, and for all of those who come after us. Whether we send a bad text, make a wrong turn, or eat something forbidden; God knows how to help us. God chose confetti to come for us by sending His son and continues to confetti us by giving us His Spirit. Jesus is our remedy, the solution to our brokenness, and the help for all of our weakness. Staying close to Him and securing ourselves in Him is our best bet when we want to hide. Thankfully Eve's story doesn't end with her hiding. She moves outside the garden with Adam, and they build a life together. They work, they build, they have kids, and I'd like to believe they find their way. Yes, one moment can mark us, but God always has a way forward.

3. Let's stop and consider some of our own marking moments and see how we've moved through them.

   a. What is something good that happened in your life that has left a mark?

   _____

   b. What else have you gone through that has left a mark on you?

   _____

   _____

   c. Have any your "marking moments" influenced how you now view God or others? Please explain.

   _____

   _____

4. What or who would you say is "leaving a mark" on you in this season of your life?

   _____

   _____

5. How else are you being marked right now? Is it by love, joy, excitement, fear, worry, etc. Are you marked by certain people, circumstances, or something the Lord is doing?

_____

I think it's important to see how certain events and people in our lives shape us because they can be a lens that we start to view life through, good or bad. How we feel and how we see can really affect what we say. For instance, my daughter Ruby rarely cleans her glasses. The other day she was beckoning a squirrel in our yard to come to her and when I asked her why she was yelling to a pinecone, she bent over and started laughing hysterically. Her view was blurry and what she was seeing was affecting what she was saying. Our perspective and our views are often based on our life experiences, and it will give us a certain lens toward God and others. Those views will have specific impact about how we cheer and applaud for others. Our views can change though, just as we can. We can clear our lens with Gods word and get intentional about how we want our lives to affect others.

6. Write a couple of things down about how you *would* like your life to "mark" others this season.

_____

_____

I think it's good to think about *how* we might want to be marking people's lives with our lives. How do we want people to feel after we leave a room or a conversation? If we want others to feel encouraged and uplifted by us, then we must be mindful about the words we're using and how we are speaking. If we want others to be marked by our generosity, then we need to be thoughtful with our actions and really listen to someone else's needs and how we might be able to help.

Marking other people usually doesn't happen accidentally, it happens because we have thought about the kind of impact we want to have on others. When we are thoughtful about *how* we want to leave a mark with others, then we can make specific steps to be the kind of people that actually leave one.

PRAYER

Today was a heavy chapter. The burden that sin and shame can leave with us doesn't always pass quickly. I want to take a little time and release things in prayer if our hearts are under the weight of anything that we're not meant to carry. Let's take a minute to let go of some things.

Say *aloud*; Lord I ask that you help me release any unnecessary weight I might be carrying right now. Would you help secure me by Your Spirit as I surrender the need to control certain scenarios, people, or future plans I have? I ask for your covering, Lord and I thank You for having covered my sin, my shame, and my guilt. Please, now cover my heart, mind, soul, spirit, and my day, as well as those I love. Cover us with Your love, peace, presence, protection and your voice.

I pray You will keep us in peace, guide our steps, and protect our relationships. Lord, will You help me be released of any guilt, shame, or condemnation I am coming under? Will you deliver me from any spiritual torment, oppression, or heaviness that's landed in my heart or my home? I cancel all assignments from the enemy over my life and allow only the love of God to infiltrate my heart and guide my steps. I release people from my debt (name any) so that un-forgiveness and resentment don't have an open door or a place to land with me. Now, Lord, I ask that the effects of any burdens, shame, or guilt will also be released from my life. I thank You for all You offered with Your life so that I can be free, forgiven, cleansed, healed, and redeemed. I claim Your work on the cross over myself, (my mind-body-soul-and spirit) and I come under Your leadership for my life. I submit myself to You today. Amen. (Feel free to continue in prayer-asking-listening-or laying things with Jesus. Physically hand Him specific burdens or shameful things that you don't want to keep with you and imagine the Lord taking them from you.)

ACTIVATE

Let's activate this idea of "leaving a mark" on someone today. What can you specifically do today that will leave a mark on someone in the way that you wrote it down? Maybe someone will be marked by your coffee delivery, or the message God will give you to text them. You could send a song that reminds you of them, send a small package to their house, or offer a compliment. Your options are endless. The idea is just to do something that's thoughtful... impactful. Let them know they are seen today. By the way, this is the art of "*throwing confetti.*" It's an intentional action to bless or bring benefit to another person.

Please write down who you'd like to impact and what action you are going to take. Please try to "activate" this in the next twenty hours.

_____

_____

DAY SIX

Offerings

After Adam and Eve take their bite and have things out with God, they relocate outside of Eden and start adding to their family. The example of their life is one of the most important lessons to understanding "our beginnings," the effects of comparison, and why being people who offer hooray is really an issue of life or death. Please start today by reading Genesis 4:1-16. Make some notes about what initially stands out to you and why.

Cain and Able are some of the first kids born after the fall. We don't know a ton about their upbringing or Adam and Eve's parenting style. What we do know is that they were each given something specific to steward. They each had a job to do, work that was unique to them. So, naturally, when it came time for them to bring their offering to God, they would offer and give to God out of their unique portion, what they had been given to steward.

This feels like a good starting point for a question. What does your offering look like to the Lord? Take a minute and write down what you have to offer to God in this season of your life. What have you been given to steward that you can offer back to God?

_____

_____

I do believe that our "offerings" vary in different seasons. At times, the Lord has asked me to "offer something up" almost like a fast for a season. I've offered Him my time, my resources, my talents, my favorite drinks, my kids, my shopping, my marriage, and ultimately, my life. I'm not just talking about offering our money or "tithe" to the Lord, ten percent of what we make naturally goes to Him. But rather, what has He given you that you can in turn offer and give back to Him? What habits have you created for yourself that He might want you to "offer up" for a season?

This might be worth asking Him if you find yourself unsure. God doesn't need anything from us, but I think it moves His heart when we are willing to actively put our wants aside and ask the Lord what He might be wanting from us. I don't think it's always "what" we are offering, it's just that when we offer, it changes our focus. Our aim is directed at what pleases Him and that will always bring us benefit.

Back to the boys. The text says that Able offered his firstborn and the fat portions to God. He brought the best of what he had, and Cain brought some of what the land produced. Ultimately God looked on Abel's offering with favor and approval but with Cain, God didn't approve. Cain holds back from God and blames His brother for offering so generously. Abel's generous offering wasn't the problem though. God was not comparing their offerings to each other. The problem was that Cain "didn't do what was right for him."

1. What do our offerings reveal about our hearts?

_____

_____

2. What causes you to "hold back" with what you have to offer the Lord? Why is that?

_____

_____

_____

Let me be so clear here; other people have nothing to do with what we have to offer. The things that we have to bring and extend to the Lord are uniquely personal. We have grace on our lives to do different things and if we start to compare our offerings and measure those offerings based on what others have to bring, then we are going to find ourselves in a heap of frustration and disappointment.

Cain doesn't spend too much time looking inside himself to deal with his pain, instead, he looks externally and seeks to blame. Cain chooses blame, a common covering for his exposure, but it's not going to hide the internal disruption he feels. There are plenty of things Cain could have chosen to "kill," like his pride or ego for instance, but it's his brother that goes to the grave.

Cains buries his own brother, partly I think, because comparison got the best of him. Clapping for others won't always feel glamorous, but it will keep us from getting our hands dirty. Anytime we try to kill what is threatening us instead of coping with the feelings that it's bringing up inside of us, we need to pause and ask, "Lord, what's going on here?" Because Cain's tendencies to kill and cover are still alive in us today. We can kill with our words, cover our motives, and then act like nothing has happened. Sorting through our feelings won't only help us but also those closest to us.

3. How do you tend to deal with disappointment or rejection?

_____

_____

_____

Listen, we are not always going to feel like clapping and cheering for one another, but that doesn't mean we don't do it. If we only did the things we "felt" like doing, none of us would get much done. Ok, I'll speak for myself, I would rarely get things done. We clap and cheer even when it hurts and pokes at our pride because celebrating another person is our way out of comparison. In fact, it's the way to kill comparison and not let it start to grow up in our lives. When God is doing a good work in someone else's life, then for goodness' sake, please clap your hands. Don't let the favor on someone else's life threaten yours, let it push you to your potential. Do "the right thing" with what God has given you to do and stay focused in that direction. It's hard enough to do what God intends for us, let alone have the time to look at what others are doing. Clap your way forward. In fact, this is a great time for an activation.

ACTIVATE

Think for a minute about who you can "clap" for today. It might not be someone you necessarily feel like celebrating, but honestly, that is the point. It is so nice when we find it easy to applaud and encourage people we love, but it doesn't build a lot of confetti muscle. There are times when our cheering will become our "offerings" to the Lord. Our clapping can cost us something; at times, our offering will be humbling or even hurtful for us. There is nothing wrong with that. In 2 Samuel 24:24, David says, "I will not bring an offering to the Lord that has cost me nothing." It will often cost us something to champion another, I don't think God minds that at all.

When you notice favor on another, then clap. When you see someone killing it, that's your cue to cheer. When you feel small because others seem so big, get out the confetti, friend! That's your invitation to partner with hooray. No one wants to walk in Cain's shoes, guilt-ridden and wandering around because he didn't know how to move past his own pain. Choose the confetti. Get out the megaphone and say something good.

   A. Please write down the name of the one you will choose to celebrate today. Please pray for them and then move toward an immediate action of something you can do to bless them.

_____

B. Your life matters and you have something good to offer. Sometimes we need a good reminder that we have plenty of things to offer to God and to others. Write down several things that you like about yourself and that you're good at. I know this practice can feel weird sometimes, but let God bring a highlighter to your own life. There will always be something we want to get better at or growth we want to have, but for now, just take a couple of minutes to bless yourself. (If this is hard for you then think about what someone else might write about you.) What are the "gifts" on your life, or ways you bring benefit to others?

_____

_____

_____

Next, Cain is removed from God's presence and is physically "marked" by this painful experience (Gen. 4:15). He lost so much more than just his brother. Let's learn from what our feelings are telling us because they will show us the *things* that need to die in us: jealousy, fear, pride, scarcity, etc. Cain chose the wrong thing to bury that day. I wonder if there is something in your own life that might need to "die" or be buried in order for you to throw confetti a little better?

4. People are not our problem; they just point to the things (or feelings) in us that we need to process. Is there any person in your life that is bringing up painful or unwanted feelings for you? What are you experiencing and what do you think that is about?

_____

_____

_____

PRAYER

Lastly, read over Psalm 139 as we close today. Read it like a prayer. Read it until something sticks with you. Let the Lord comb through your heart and see if He wants to surface, speak, or comfort you. Sometimes we don't always know how we "feel" or what's beneath the surface. Life has a way of numbing us at times, it's good practice to go to the God who knows us completely. He knows why we do the things we do. He knows how and why we choose to conceal. He knows the reason for our pain, our points of pride, and where we get tripped up. Thankfully, He also knows the way through all that. He knows where we need healing and how to get it. He knows the path we can take to get us back to Himself and He knows the people to place us next to as we walk that road.

Write down what stands out to you out in Psalm 139.

_____

_____

_____

_____

MEDITATION

"You have encircled me, you have placed your hand on me." (Psalm 139:5)

DAY SEVEN

Shine

In the book *Throwing Confetti*, I talk in chapter two about coming out of hiding, because it's hard to throw confetti when we're staying hidden. *Capes and Camouflage* is about how and why we hide. We touched on this a little bit as we observed Adam and Eve, and now we're going to look at a few more examples of where people liked to hide, how they came out, and what helped them along the way.

We know that being made in God's image, we are a people created to reflect Him and shine. Anytime we choose to hide ourselves or conceal certain parts ourselves, we are dimming our light. We mask the brilliance that Christ has put within us, and less light is offered in the world. It's hard to radiate hope or offer confetti if we stay concealed. Let's start by looking at a couple verses that would call us to come forth and speak to the purpose of us *being* light. Please read them and write down a few words that stand out to you.

1. **Isaiah 60:1**

2. **Mathew 5:15-15**

3. **John 8:12**

4. **Psalm 18:28**

5. **Micah 7:8**

1. What is the intended purpose of light?

_____

2. Do you feel free to shine brilliantly? Why or why not?

_____

3. What keeps you or can keep you from shining?

_____

The definition of light reveals that it carries energy. It is the primary tool for perceiving the world and communicating with it. Light warms the earth, improves visibility, reduces fatigue, affects our mood, and improves work productivity. Without light, there would be no sight. Light shows people the way. Light is also controlled by a specific source. A light switch or a lamp can have a dimmer that turns on or turns down the light. I think all of us have internal sources we are connected to that allow us to "turn up" our light and if it is not "connected" properly then we will stay dim.

1. Can you identify some of your "internal switches" that factor into how brightly you shine? (Who/What/etc.)

_____

One of the ways Jesus identifies His children is by calling us "light." We are the light of the world. Labels are important, they speak to our identity. For me personally, I love to start the week or the month by asking the Lord what label or name He wants to call me. How does He want to address me? How does He want to engage with me this week/this season? I'm finding that what He says about me is often tied to what He wants me to do. For instance, light requires us to be bright, to shine. If God is addressing me as "light," I'd then reflect to make sure I am shining. I would look at anything that might be keeping my light hidden, and I would keep that at the forefront of my mind wherever I'm going for the week. I would be intentional about shining while I'm interacting, parenting, conversing, buying groceries, etc.

This is one way we can allow Jesus to be hooray for us. We can ask Him how He sees us and what He wants to say to us. I then google the name He gives me. I look up what the purpose is for that name, and I say a prayer and ask the Holy Spirit to help me understand and connect with that name. It's been more than a sweet practice; it's secured and strengthened me. It's helped me come out of places of hiding because when we know who we are, what God thinks of us, and what He's calling us to, it's really hard to stay hidden.

Let's give this a shot…

ACTIVATE

There's no pressure on you. Your only job is to present yourself before the Lord. Get someplace quiet so that it feels easier to hear the whisper. Ask the Holy Spirit to speak and enlighten you as to what He's saying. Deuteronomy 29:29 says, "The secret things belong to the Lord our God, but the things revealed belong to us and to our children forever." There are things He wants to reveal to you. Write it down, look it up, and reflect on how this word over you will cause you to posture yourself differently in your day. Write down the name that He's speaking over you. How will that affect you this week?

_____

_____

_____

DAY EIGHT

Giants

My husband loves to hunt and recently, he's been taking our son, Asher, with him. They dress strategically when they go out, putting on camouflage to try to blend into their surroundings. It makes me think of the different ways that we too can camouflage ourselves in our everyday lives. It's really less about what we wear and more about how we show up.

We're about to read a passage about a man named David. David was a shepherd who turned King, but there's a lot that happens before David sits on his throne. Today, we're going to read about a grocery delivery that David was asked to make and see how his errands turned into a rescue mission. Please read 1 Samuel 17: 1-57. I promise it's worth your read, highlight anything that stands out to you.

1. David was just another guy in the sea of men that day, offering his light but still blending in, no doubt. What do you think made David different than the others?

_____

David chose to *act* differently by choosing to, in fact, act. One act made David stand out and shine while all the others stayed put. It can be vulnerable, letting your light shine. It can feel scary letting other people see your strength. They accuse, misunderstand your motives, attack your identity, and feel like they have the right to offer an opinion about the places you're going. If you are going to shine this season, you're going to have to put all that behind you. The opinions of others will keep you from shining and offering what you have. No one was offering confetti for David and if he had held back, he wouldn't have been the nation's hero. His courage released confetti to fall for God's people and no one had expected it.

2. Is there something you need to "put behind you" in order to step forward? (David had to move past his brother's insults and Saul's opinions in order to step forward.) Are there accusations, or misunderstandings from others that you need to put aside, give to God, and really let go of in order to move more confidently?

_____

3. What are some of your responsibilities in this season? Remember, David was just running an errand, bringing bread to his brothers. He was being obedient to what his dad had asked of him and then he found himself in the middle of a battle. His obedience led to everyone's breakthrough. Sometimes, it's just good to remind ourselves that the mundane provides countless opportunities for the miraculous to happen. Be thoughtful and alert as you go about your daily business, you never know who might need your words, your faith, or your actions as you shine.

_____

_____

4. Goliath yelled and threatened, and it pushed David to go to the front of the line. Goliath's intimidation tactics ended up being David's invitation to promotion. I believe this is a preview of how God wants us to view the giants in our lives, they can actually propel us instead of hindering us. Any place where we feel intimidated and threatened can actually be an open door for something greater in our lives. Are you currently facing any giants, something that feels threatening or intimidating to you? What effect is it having?

_____

_____

5. David used an unlikely weapon against his enemy, but it proved to be the perfect weapon for Goliath's weakness. Sometimes, what we have in our arsenal doesn't look like much, but because we've trained with it, it's really comfortable for us. I think it's important for us to take stock of what we already have been equipped with. What are some of the "weapons" you have been given/ strengths you have?

_____

_____

6. Ok, all this can sound really good, our enemies providing a platform for our promotion and so on, but I know that enemies have a way of seriously squelching us. Often for me, my voice will feel hindered, and I can feel stuck, unable to move forward. But if I can make it to my knees to offer

a prayer, turn my ear to the Holy Spirit, and enlist some friends to speak truth to me, then it can bring me back to God's lens and perspective. I realize that our time here is short, that this is only our training ground for what's eternally ahead for us, and that each "giant" I face develops more muscle for me. How have your "giants" have helped or developed you?

_____

_____

Saul wants David to put on armor and fight like all of the others. Armor can protect us, but it can also hide us. If David had been hidden and hindered, he wouldn't have been able to offer his strength and move so freely. I think that's why it's important to note *how* God has developed us and the things He has uniquely given us because confetti comes in all forms. Other leaders (Saul) can offer advice, but it's important that we only take hold of what's suited for us. I guess this is less of a question and more of an observation, I just want to make sure we aren't wearing any armor that's not meant for us. Not all armor actually protects people.

ACTIVATION

I'd like to close today with prayer. All this talk about giants can sometimes be a little triggering and if you're in the middle of a "standoff" against an enemy right now, you need a divine approach. God's strategy often looks different than ours. He says to "Love our enemies and pray for those persecuting us" (Math.5:44). He does fit us for our battles though. Ephesians 6:12 says that our real enemies are not against those with flesh and blood. Since our *real* enemies are spiritual entities, we need to fight them strategically. Please look up Ephesians 6:10-18 and write down what each piece of armor stands for and then ask the Lord what "weapon" He might be instructing you to really focus on as you dress yourself spiritually. This is a good daily practice. Surrender your imagination unto the Lord and really picture the pieces of armor as you put them on.

DAY NINE

More Measuring

We are going to stick to the 1 Samuel 17 text for one more day. This passage is loaded with insightful lessons for us. Today, we are going to look at some of Goliath's tactics and a little more of David's backstory to see what we can learn.

1. In 1 Sam.17:37, David makes a statement before he goes out to meet Goliath, a declaration really, about how he's going to defeat the giant. I love it, because at this point David doesn't know that he will slay Goliath, but he has all the confidence that it will happen. Write down what he says.

_____

_____

_____

2. I think it's important for us to make declarations. It's a good way to position ourselves for the day. Whether we are getting ready for a meeting, bowing our head in prayer, speaking truth over our kids, or like David, about to change a nation, truth gives us confidence and creates paths for our feet to walk on. Write down a couple of declaration statements that you need for today. Write down what you need to hear in order to walk confidently throughout your day. Write until you feel the confetti falling… (If you need some help getting started, try this; today I have all that I need. I have a Father in Heaven with unlimited resources to supply me with every need. I have the courage to….)

_____

_____

_____

3. The reason why something feels like a "giant" typically is because we are comparing it to something smaller. If David had compared himself to Goliath and had the same measuring system as the other men, it's possible he would have stayed back and held back what was his to offer. David has another means of measuring though; he gives us a clue in 1 Sam. 17:37. His declaration is his truth. Who does David measure Goliath by?

___

4. God is a good measuring system for any believer of Jesus. If we are making our measurements based on who God is and what He can do, then measuring won't really matter because, with God, we always have the upper hand. We have to do our part to train and steward what God gives us, so that when God decides it's our turn to magnify who He is in our life, then we will be ready. Look at a passage in 2 Kings 6:8-23. We can't measure things by "normal" standards, the things we see. When we are only looking at what's in the "natural," we won't always feel encouraged. We need to see what God is seeing, hear what God is saying, and then partner with what He's asking us to do next. What are your tendencies when something is threatening your security?

___

___

It's important to make note of our responses when we feel threatened. Some of us get paralyzed and want to hide, while others of us want to rush towards the oncoming traffic. It's that flight, fight, or freeze thing. I tend to run towards the battle if it's big enough, it's the smaller things that can get me. Death by a thousand blows. I tolerate and tolerate and then I tend to isolate. But when the giants are big and the enemy is yelling loudly, then let me at them. I know how to position myself for that kind of enemy. I know who has my back and I know He has the solution to every problem I am facing. How about for you? Does God feel like the solution for what you need? Why or why not?

___

___

5. It seems like everywhere I look throughout the Bible, the choice to compare is a real one. They had to decide if they would partner with God and who He was or choose to act on what they saw. This

is important when it comes to confetti throwing because comparison can easily take you out and keep you hidden. Worry, fear, inadequacies, all these things blur our view and keep us from taking any steps forward. Your hooray will dwindle, and your voice can get quiet if you think you need to somehow "measure up" to something. The giants get bigger, and we feel smaller, but the truth is that we have God behind us, tipping the scale. You should be comparing God next to the thing that you want to do, you want to say, where you want to go, etc. And then like David, go about your day and step into what God opens up for you.

We should pause and reflect here. Is there any place in your life that you need to bring God into the equation as you make your measurement? What is it and how does factoring God into your equation tip the scale for you?

_____

_____

_____

_____

PRAYER

I feel the need to end today by praying for the kind of boldness and bravery that David had. I think the only way to come out of hiding is to really *believe* that God has us. That He sees us, hears us, secures us, and comes to our aid. Would you hold out your hands in front of you and ask for the Lord to impart to you a kind of holy boldness? Courage that would take on a lion, a bear, and any threatening giant. A faith that would believe for God's outcome no matter what you're looking at, a strength that will not only make you a hero, but will help set others free and bring blessing to them. Pray that you will have a security so rooted in God that it will cause you to act when others hold back. Pray for a tender dependency on the Holy Spirit to obey His leading, even when it doesn't make sense, and that you will have an anointing to conquer anything in your way. Pray that when giants see you coming, they will turn the other way.

DAY TEN

Baggage

We know that sin, certain giants, and other people can try to keep us in hiding. Today we're going to look at how our personal assignments and old baggage can try to keep us in hiding too.

Before Saul was named Israel's first King, they had to pull him out of "baggage" so that he could take his place. It's a beautiful story about how hooray and confetti call people out of hiding and help others go higher. Please read 1 Samuel 10:1-27 where Saul gets anointed for what's next. If you want to back up and start with chapter nine, you won't be sorry.

In verse sixteen, Saul is already hiding the call of God on his life from His uncle. We could speculate about why, but it's hard to say for sure. Maybe he was still getting used to the idea, maybe he was afraid his uncle wouldn't agree with his new assignment to be king. Maybe he felt like he was bragging about it, or maybe he just didn't want to process what that meant for him. Whatever the reason, Saul is not sharing the information, he's hiding it.

1. What are some reasons why you might hide who you are from others? We can hide physically; we can emotionally hide our hearts and not be vulnerable. We can hide our intellect or intellectually hide behind the things we know. We can hide the gifts we have or what God gives us to carry. Truth be told, we can hide in all kinds of ways for all kinds of reasons. What's typical of you?

_____

_____

The new King Saul is hiding among the baggage (Samuel 10:22). Baggage is a good physical picture with a lot of symbolic meaning. Baggage can keep us stuck, hidden, and make it hard for us to step into our roles. I was just at the store the other day looking for new "carry-on" luggage for some traveling. The baggage came in all kinds of sizes, shapes, and colors. They had different compartments and ways to carry them. I think the same is true of our personal "baggage" that we carry with us from our past. Sometimes, the things we carry with us are heavy, adding a lot of weight to us. Some of our baggage is complex or compartmentalized, we all carry our baggage differently. Most of our baggage is unseen though, it sits in our minds as memories, or it's tucked in our hearts and packaged neatly.

2. Is there any baggage from your past that still has you hiding?

_____

_____

For Saul, the baggage was a good hiding place. Who knows how long he would have stayed there if hooray hadn't helped him up? Here's what I mean; Saul found his way out because of the words spoken by others. This is why I think *hooray* is so life-changing. We can help others take their place by offering a good word or a kind act. When someone doesn't know the way forward, or is just stuck for a minute, all we really need to do is get close to them. Close enough for them to hear our words, feel our presence, and see that our hands are clapping, not finger-pointing. That's how we make confetti fall.

There are people around us who are stuck in baggage. People who need our presence and words of encouragement. Who knows who could take their place because of what you might have to say? We'll have to make a choice to act honorably in these situations because as Saul's story shows us, criticism would have been an easy option. Thankfully, some of the people that surrounded Saul thought more about helping him instead of adding to the things that hindered him. They chose not to hide what they had to offer and because of that, a King took his place.

3. I wonder to myself what words they used when they ran and found Saul. What did they say to bring the first King out of hiding? Shame, anger, insults; these are not helpful tools to call people up and into more. I bet they echoed words like "you can do this" and "we will be with you." Whatever the words were, they landed with Saul. Their help became the path for his feet to walk and confetti covered his steps as he walked out of hiding and took his place.

What do you typically need when you are having a hard time dealing with something?

_____

_____

4. In 1 Sam. 10:24 it reads, "Do you see the one the Lord has chosen? There is not a man like him among the entire population. And all the people shouted, 'Long live the King.'"

What a way to describe Saul, not a man like him around. That doesn't sound like a man who would be hiding in baggage, but often, what's being said about us isn't always what we say about ourselves. Take a minute and write down some good words about yourself. Maybe some new ones. Words the Lord might say or something others have said.

_____

_____

ACTIVATION

I think it's important to practice partnering with hooray. Just like the people in 1 Sam. 10:23 who ran (with some words) and pulled Saul out, let's see who the Lord might put in our hearts to help today. Reflect, pray, and consider who stands out to you. What you could offer them? Is there a text to send, a note to drop, or something else you can do to offer hooray on their behalf? On a side note, if you're the one currently feeling stuck in the corner, then consider how being hooray for *yourself* might help you out. Write down some thoughts, feelings, struggles, or wonderings of any kind. Let's see if any action is needed, and you can write that down too. Maybe it would be helpful to join a small group like a prayer group, see a counselor, or start going for walks with a friend. There could be any number of things to do. Don't worry about that part though, just start with reflection and see what comes up.

_____

_____

_____

DAY ELEVEN

Protection

Webster's Dictionary defines "hiding" as: a place to seek protection, to conceal for shelter, to keep secret, to screen from something, or put out of sight. There are plenty of places for us to hide, but really only one proper hiding place. Today, we are going to read through a couple of different passages and make sure we are only hiding in places that really help us. Please start by reading through a couple of Psalms and writing down what stands out to you. Read Psalm 17, 27, and 32. Then choose one of the Psalms to answer your questions about.

1. What words describe God as a hiding place?

_____

2. Why was David (the author of the psalm) in hiding?

_____

3. Would you describe God as a hiding place for you? Why or why not?

_____

4. Do your hideouts bring you more solace or security?

_____

Sometimes we are hiding *from* something and sometimes we need to tuck in to hide *for* something. For example, God had almost put David in "hiding" while he was taking care of sheep. He wasn't hiding necessarily, but he was hidden from the outside world. He was working, learning lessons, and in training for what he would step into. I remember a season when I felt like God was "hiding" me. I was staying at home while my kids were little, and though I felt thankful for my time with them, I also wanted to be stepping into some other things and using my talents in other ways.

That season was important for so many reasons. It was in that season that I taught my kids how to pray and hear from God. I used easy language and developed tools to share with them that I'm still using today. I still teach the same strategy to our staff and others. That season of "hiding" proved to be super helpful, not only for me, but also for the people who get to benefit because of the season that I felt "concealed."

PRAYER

God is a safe place of refuge and for us as followers of Christ, I believe we too should imitate Him and be a refuge and safe place for others. Isaiah 32 isn't necessarily talking about us personally, but I've adopted it personally for myself. "Each will be like a shelter from the wind, a refuge from the rain" (Isa. 32:2). I think if we want to be people who carry confetti with us and use our voices to echo hooray, we must be the kind of people that come out of hiding and that help hide others from the storms they face. So, I've been praying a simple prayer lately, "God, would you help make me a safe person, a shelter in the storms?"

That's not a long prayer or an eloquent one, but it's proved to be very powerful, maybe even a little painful if I'm honest. God will expose the parts of you that are not safe for others. He will highlight an attitude, a thought pattern, lies you believe, etc. But if we are serious about wholeness, healing, and helping people, then this is a prayer you will want to adopt for yourself. Yes, we can still be hooray and offer confetti, even if we aren't whole, healed, and totally "safe," but why wait for Heaven to inherit all that? Let's do hard work now so there is a great benefit on this side of eternity for us and for those next to us.

I sincerely pray that your whole self will come out of hiding this season. I pray that you will not mask any part of who you are, because you are needed. May you shine brightly and always offer your light in the places God puts you.

ACTIVATE

Would you be brave enough to ask God to reveal any "unsafe" places in your life?

MEDITATION

"Arise, shine, for your light has come, and the glory of the Lord shines over you" (Isaiah 60:2).

DAY TWELVE

Booray

Today we are going to be sorting out our boo. That's right, our boo. If "hooray" is a spirit we can have, then "booray" is one too. Yes, I made up the word, but it seems to really fit. Boo can be a touchy subject but it's vital we look inside ourselves and see what's tripping us up. Shame and feeling bad won't help us in our observations, so let's make a deal to comb through this stuff with no guilt or "I'm really failing" mantras. Let's just look honestly and wade into this topic carefully. Let me start by telling you what boo can do.

Boo belittles, minimizes, tears down, and holds back applause. Hooray is about building up and cheering for others and booray goes against all that. Booray can pop up in your life at different times and for all different reasons. I believe we all have it to some extent. There's not a "one size fits all" solution because the struggle is uniquely different. You could have a lack of understanding about your identity and that may cause you to feel threatened, intimidated, and caught up in comparison to those around you. You might feel like you have to put others down or hold back from extending toward others in order for you to feel good. You might feel like people don't deserve your hooray; policing and judging them to your personal set of standards. You could have grown up in a household where it was the norm to belittle or compete. Yikes, did I mention this might be touchy? Friend, if it feels easy or natural for you to extend a complaint or criticism to others, then you might just have a problem with boo.

You can see that in order to partner with hooray, it's imperative that we sort through some of the reasons that hold us back. Let's start by doing a little digging by way of reflection. Write down a couple of reasons why you might find it difficult to celebrate another person. What would cause you to hold back your cheer, compliments, prayer, or encouragement for them?

There are a couple of approaches to dealing with our boo. I think the best one might be to walk up on it real slow, almost like we are trying to get close to a wild animal. We could look at a couple of Bible texts, make way for some reflection, and see what God shows us. But if you are bent more towards a shotgun approach, then let me give it to you straight. Boo can be more than just a negative bend in us, it can be a spirit that we are dealing with, typically a spirit of accusation, rejection, or jealousy. And if it's a "spirit problem" then no amount of reflecting and reading will get rid of the booray in our lives. We will need to ask that spirit to leave and then clean house so that it's gone for good. But first things first, let's see where the problem lies. Answer these next couple of questions and be really honest with yourself, no one else is going to see this.

1. Do you feel like you want to say something encouraging or complimentary but just can't for some reason? You can't really explain why, it's just that nothing seems to come out when you try.

   _____

2. Do you find it difficult to pray for others? Not because you don't know what words to say but because your voice feels locked up or constricted somehow?

   _____

3. Do you immediately assess yourself when you notice something nice or admirable in another?

   _____

4. Does it feel bad or even painful for you when others are being highlighted or talked about in an encouraging way?

   _____

5. Are you discrediting people either out loud by way of gossip, or quietly in your head?

   _____

6. Do you tend to decide quickly (judgmentally) why someone can't be your friend or have plenty of reasons why you won't get close to someone?

   _____

Ok, if you have answered yes to most of these questions, then you could be dealing with a spirit. Spirits are addressed all throughout the Bible and the way we get rid of them is to pray. It's typically called "deliverance" but not everyone feels comfortable with that word, we've all seen too many bad movies that make deliverance look scary and feel like it's for "really messed up" people. Deliverance means there is rescue, relief, escape, or freedom that happens for us. It's an essential part of the ministry that Jesus came to do so that we could experience wholeness and relief from dark influences in our lives (Luke 4:17-22, Isaiah 61:1-2, Math.

8:28-9:1, Mark 5:1-21, Luke 8:26-40, for some reference). We see Jesus bring healing and deliverance to many after he would get done preaching. Likewise, it's part of what Jesus asks us to do for those that follow him.

7. Please read Mark 16:15-19 and Luke 9:1-2. Then write down what Jesus said to do and what signs would follow those who believe.

_____

_____

8. In Isaiah 61:1, Jesus says that He came to set captives and prisoners free. A captive is taken by force (didn't do anything wrong) and a prisoner did something to deserve being imprisoned. Whether we "deserved" something or not, Jesus comes for all of us and issues freedom on our behalf. Is there a place in your life where you feel like you are "held captive" or being "imprisoned" by something? Please explain.

_____

_____

ACTIVATE

This feels like a great time to activate a deliverance prayer over us. Too many of us have bad theology about what it means to be "possessed" by demons. In the Greek, the word "possessed" means afflicted or harassed. Many followers of Jesus are "afflicted" by evil spirits for various reasons. We can open a door for the enemy to harass us because of sin, things we do, what we watch, being entertained by evil, opening ourselves up to spiritually dark things outside the realm of Jesus, etc.

If you haven't prayed to be delivered (relieved or rescued) it might seem strange but try to give it a shot anyway, you won't have anything to lose. I've made it a practice for myself because I don't need any "outside source" interfering with my mind, heart, or emotions. Life is hard enough without the help of dark entities trying to harass or influence us.

If you feel comfortable, take some time and ask God if you are "under the influence" of anything other than His Holy Spirit. We can often tell what spirit it is by the fruit of it. For example, if you feel jealous, it can be a spirit of jealousy, if angry, we can have a spirit of anger. Jesus commanded spirits to leave by the name that was often plaguing the person (a deaf or mute sprit was causing someone to be deaf or mute. You can find that evidence in Mark 9:25).

I usually play some soft music, grab my anointing oil, and then ask the Lord what is "afflicting" me. Next, I put my hands on my stomach, heart, or head (depending on where the harassment is coming from) and then I command any dark and foul spirit to leave. It's helpful to repent for opening any doors (Lord, I repent for my involvement in….), then vocally close any doors that you opened (I now close all doors that have been opened in my life that gave that spirit room and access, to bother, and harass me). Renounce the spirit from having any access to you (I renounce the spirit of…from being able to work any longer and I cut off all ties and legal access that this spirit had, and I command it to leave now and never return, in Jesus' name). And it would be wise to keep those doors closed so that we don't allow any further affliction over ourselves. By the way, this is helpful if we are feeling "afflicted" in any area. I heard someone once say, "We can't crucify what needs to be delivered in our life and we can't deliver what needs to be crucified." Meaning, some things need to leave our lives through prayer and some things need to be handled through discipline and making good choices.

If you have people that you trust and feel safe with or pray with regularly, then it's not a bad idea to invite other people into the process. A good reference for praying specific kinds of prayers is John and Staci Eldridge. He has a daily prayer, a prayer for deliverance, a "life" prayer, a bedtime prayer, inner healing prayers, breaking curses, and more. His "wild at heart" app is free and loaded with helpful tools. Go ahead and give it a listen. You won't be sorry.

DAY THIRTEEN

Getting Rid Of Your Boo

If a "spirit of boo" is not your problem, then we need to address your boo in a different way. Write down all the reasons why people don't need your applause. I do mean **all** of the reasons, really look at what comes up for you. Make a list about why you don't need to clap for people, why they don't need your voice, and why it's ok for you to hold back. I'll leave plenty of room.

_____

_____

_____

1. Do you believe that you don't have anything to offer or that some people don't deserve to receive what you have? Where do you think your feelings are coming from?

_____

_____

2. Mathew 10:5-8 tells us that we have been "given freely" so we need to "give freely." This command has nothing to do with how we feel, what sort of knowledge we have, or the gifts we've been given. God's word doesn't say that we should only give to others if they are deserving of our voice/time/efforts. He just says to give, and to give freely. We give unto Him and as we extend to others, we end up blessing the Lord. How could this kind of posture change how you interact with others?

_____

_____

Our boo is coming from someplace. Maybe a place of un-forgiveness or bitterness. You could be dealing with rejection in your relationships. Sometimes, if you feel rejected by people, you could be rejecting others. Your boo could be from tiredness, selfishness, small mindedness, pride, or forgetfulness. You just simply might not be making an intentional effort to throw confetti and cheer for others. Maybe boo isn't your real problem, maybe it's a lack of effort or "know-how." Whatever the case is, we usually already know, in part, what the solution could be. Write down a couple of things you *could* do in order to come out of your boo.

_____

_____

3. We are going to read today about John the Baptist. John was Jesus' cousin. John was the one who was sent ahead of Jesus to prepare people's hearts for his arrival. If you don't know the story, it doesn't end well. Please read today about the last conversation Jesus has with John and then let's make some observations. Read Luke 7:18-30

_____

_____

Sometimes our boo feels justified. Someone has hurt us, or we feel betrayed. We don't get the solution we want, or maybe we've lost hope in people, or in some way we've lost some hope in God coming through in the way we'd like. Our circumstances sure have a way of bringing out the boo in us.

I want to point out that when John asks Jesus a question, Jesus brings the answer back to John's prison. He is still answering us inside our own prisons, by the way. Some people feel imprisoned by their marriages, their finances, circumstances, sin, etc. I want to assure you that Jesus has something to say to you even if you're feeling locked up somehow.

So, I'm wondering if there is a question you need to ask Jesus. Maybe it's about yourself or someone else. A conversation with the King might not be the full resolution to your pain, or your boo, but it sure can't hurt. We don't need to beg for Him to speak, we are simply coming (and we have a right to come as His child) and we are asking our "Father" for help. Let's wrap up today by taking a couple of minutes in a listening prayer and asking the Holy Spirit what He would like to say to you. What does He want to address with your heart today concerning your boo? (He will be gentle, I'm sure of it. So, relax, get quiet, and lean in.)

ACTIVATE

Write down one thing you WILL DO today to stop partnering with boo. If you are short on solutions, let me suggest a few things. Is there a verse you could write out, memorize, and hang up someplace? Renewing our minds and changing our thoughts is an avenue toward clapping our hands. Could you come at your boo in the "opposite spirit" and choose to activate hooray today by making a phone call, sending a card, or doing something kind for someone? Could you confess to someone that it's hard for you to practice hooray and that you might need some help staying accountable to stop speaking poorly of people? You could ask God to increase your lens for "others" and try to focus more on their needs than on your own. The list could go on and on.

In truth, if you're stuck in boo then it's probably helping you in some way. It's keeping you protected from having to offer yourself. It's positioning you in a certain way, allowing you to justify staying still or staying on top, depending on how your boo is manifesting. But if you're really wanting to get rid of it, then you'll do something about it. What action can you take today to stop your boo from getting the best of you?

DAY FOURTEEN

What's Really Going On

I know sorting through our boo can be a little difficult. Shame and guilt can start to creep in, and our hearts can become an easy target for lies to land. So, let's be careful here that we don't take on the role of a victim, feel helpless to change, or beat ourselves up in this process. It's brave to look inward. It takes courage to sort through things that keep us locked up or limited, we all need God's help to go forward to change. Healing and hooray will be on the other side of all of this, and I promise you, life is more fun with your hands clapping.

Today we are going to read through all of 1 Samuel 18.

1. Why do you think David's success was so intimidating for Saul?

_____

2. What is your response to others (the people that are close to you) when they are succeeding and things for them are favorable?

_____

Saul could have chosen to be a mentor to David and partner with him, instead he chose to be his enemy. This is a terribly hard chapter for me, primarily because this "Saul complex" is keeping so many of us from entering into divine partnerships. People and their "gifts" are so often God's gift to us. If we're not careful, we can weaponize people's strength and become so internally focused that we miss the opportunity to love, learn from, and partner with them. Jealousy is truly such a tragedy.

3. Saul's jealousy had burned so intensely it turned into dread (1 Sam. 18:15) and then into a "murderous spirit" (1 Sam.18:25) where he plots to kill David. Our feelings are good servants but terrible masters for us. Saul doesn't just internalize his feelings for David, he starts acting on them. Our feelings need to be looked at, processed, and then dealt with accordingly so that we don't end

up doing something we regret. Are there currently any feelings affecting you (or affecting how you relate to others) that you need to deal with? Write down what's surfacing.

_____

_____

4. After reading about Saul and David, please access your own relationships. Is there someone in your life you need to move closer to this season? What could be restricting you?

_____

_____

_____

PRAYER

I think it's important to sit with God in prayer and ask him to help you handle/heal emotions that need to be surrendered to Him. Negative emotions are not necessarily bad, they are giving us information that can prove helpful to us. However, if we indulge them instead of submit them, we could end up like Saul. Chasing people down and attacking who they are is a sure way to stay stuck in boo. One of the ways we can submit our feelings/frustrations to God concerning others, is to "bless our enemies." It's gross, I know (I'm kidding). This type of surrender is painful sometimes. It's an act of hooray, a "sacrificial offering," and it's one way to start counteracting our boo. Read over the words from Mathew 5:44-45 and then go ahead and give it a try. Pray for your "problem" person and pray for your own heart too.

DAY FIFTEEN

Honor

If you're still stuck in some boo, then I want to reassure you, this will get easier. If you are bringing your heart before God, dealing with the feelings that surface, and taking steps toward being able to applaud, you will get there. You will be able to bless, champion, and cheer for even the tough ones. I have plenty of stories that I could tell you about people that I found it hard to clap for, actually in full disclosure, I could barely choke out a prayer that didn't sound like, "Wow Jesus, I guess if you think this person should be a recipient of love, blessing, and care…even after all the gossip, pain, and meanness then go ahead I guess and bless them." I'm laughing now, but it was the best I could do at the time.

People are complex and none of us are perfect. It's ok to have "boo days," but when those days turn into weeks, or months, it could eventually turn into a "boo lifestyle."

Thankfully, there is a cure. Jesus is still the healer of all hearts, and the Bible is the best compass for our complexities. Today we are going to take some notes from Saul's son Jonathan and learn how humility and honor can guide us toward hooray. Feel free to familiarize yourself with 1 Samuel 18 again.

1. What struck you/stood out as you read about Jonathan?

___

___

2. Jonathan doesn't have the same lens as his dad (Saul) and therefore doesn't see David as Saul sees him. How we see people affects our response to them. What action does Jonathan take toward David and what can we learn from this?

___

___

3. Scripture says that "Jonathan loved David as much as he loved himself" (1 Sam. 18:1-3), and I believe that's what enabled him to take an action of honor and pull David close. I think God knits our hearts so close with some people that it actually doesn't feel like work to honor, bless, and champion them. Jonathan was God's solution for David when Saul was against him, and I think God still does that today. Write down some people God has placed in your life that feel like God's "answer" to you. Bless them today and remind them how grateful you are for their friendship. If you're in need, then pray for a "Jonathan" in your life. Ask God who *you* might be called to be a Jonathan for. What would that look like for you?

_____

_____

ACTIVATE

Jonathan removes his honor. That's not a typo. The robe, tunic, and armor displayed his place in the Kingdom and was part of his protection. His clothes covered him and represented strength on him. Think about what he did for a minute. He removed his importance, piece by piece, and placed it on his friend, on the one his dad would try to assassinate time and time again. It's extremely symbolic.

If we are going to be in close covenant relationships with people, we will have to remove things that cover, protect, and at times, promote us. Is there something you need to "remove" today in order to honor and move into a closer relationship with someone? In your imagination and maybe even physically, "take off" what is needed in order to move closer. Next, is there something you need to "extend" to another person that would be helpful in your relationship? Jonathan gave David something physical that he was wearing that was symbolic of his love, trust, and covenant with him. What does your offering/extension look like? Then seal this up in a time of prayer and ask the Lord how you can "cover" your friend today with your words and actions. Write down what's coming up for you.

_____

_____

DAY SIXTEEN

Humility

I can't stop thinking about Jonathan. His life is uncanny in a culture that wants so much for themselves. To give away is not the norm, or at least it's not my norm unless I'm surrendered and aligned with what Jesus has for me on the daily. I'd encourage you to read through the first four verses of 1 Samuel 18 again and ask God to graciously give you a mind and lens like Jonathan had. It will help usher hooray into your life.

1. After doing your work the last couple of days, how would you assess your "boo?" Be specific.

   _____

2. I hope by now your heart is feeling lighter and your boo is getting easier to articulate and deal with. After your assessment, are there any further steps you need to take to deal with anything that has surfaced in your heart?

   _____

3. Who is currently benefiting from what your life has to offer? I ask because sometimes in the midst of the day-to-day, things run together and get blurry. I think it's important to remember that even if we feel like our boo takes over sometimes or celebrating seems hard for us, the truth is that people are still the recipients of what your life has to offer them. So, who is benefiting from your life?

   _____

I'd like to end by having you read 1 Peter 5:6. Boo is hard to get rid of, but humility will help us. Humility has many benefits in our lives, one being that as we lower ourselves, God is responsible for the heavy lifting. Let it all go today, get lighter, get closer to Jesus, give Him your boo, and start clapping for the hard ones. It's easier when your eyes are focused on Jesus and your heart is surrendered to Him.

MEDITATION
"Humble yourselves, therefore, under God's mighty hand, that he may lift you up in due time." -Peter 5:6

DAY SEVENTEEN

Hearing God

Alright friends, hopefully by now we have determined that we want to use our life to bless and build others up. We've looked at the ways we sometimes hide, we've tried to get a handle on our boo, and today we are going to focus on hearing from God because the best way to get through the hard stuff really comes from knowing what God is saying to us. Throwing confetti comes a whole lot easier when we're next to God and we are hearing what He is saying.

1. Write down what you believe about the voice of God. Can you hear Him? Do you believe He still speaks today? Do you have concerns about it, etc.?

   _____

   _____

2. Hebrews 5:14 tells us that we can "discern" God through our different senses. Our senses provide a unique opportunity to hear from the Holy Spirit in different ways. My husband has a strong "gut" with the Lord, he typically "just feels and knows" what God is saying or asking. I rely more on my "hearing" (His whisper or His word) or "seeing" (dreams, pictures, songs, symbolism, etc.) How do you typically hear from God and what senses do you usually rely on?

   _____

3. Please look up and write down what these passages tell us when it comes to how we can "hear" from God.

   a. 2 Corinthians 2:10

   _____

   b. Habakkuk 2:1

   _____

c. Job 33:14-18

d. 2 Timothy 3:16

e. John 10:1-4

ACTIVATE

The *only* requirement to hear from God comes from John 10:1-4, we must be His. If we are His, then we *can* hear from Him. You may not be used to it, you might need some practice with it, but rest assured, you can certainly do it. My kids didn't know anything about me when they were babies, but they could still hear and respond to my voice. He speaks and we are only responsible to listen. So, I'd love for us to "activate our senses" and spiritually turn them on and tune them into hearing God. Think for a minute, what "sense" would you like God to speak to you through (hearing, seeing, tasting, smelling, feeling,)? Once you know, focus on that specific sense hopefully it's one you're not used to using with the Lord) and then pray. Ask God to "speak" in a specific way and write down your experience.

PRAYER

Father, I am here to be with you. Would you activate and turn on my senses in a new way? Get creative and turn up the volume. Go overboard and help me to discern that it's you and your voice. I silence all other voices, including my own and I ask that you release encouragement or whatever else you have for me in full measure today. What would you like to say to me Lord?

DAY EIGHTEEN

Lean In

Hearing God is an incredible privilege for the children of God. His voice changes everything. We don't use it as a weapon (God told me this "thing" about you) or as manipulation. His voice isn't a "trump" card (God said we *have* to do this), but we rely on His speaking as guidance, connection, and revelation in our lives. It helps us to bless and encourage others about what's in and on God's heart for them. We hear by faith, we hold onto His words with faith, and then we extend and release those words to others through our faith. Today I want to look at a couple of things that God's word does and then we will practice hearing and extending His word.

In Psalm 107:20 it says, "He sent his word and healed them." One of the things God's word does is bring healing. There have been so many times in my life that I have needed a word from God to bring me some healing. Healing in my perspective, healing to usher in hope, healing to my heart when it has been hurt. I get healing knowing that He's hearing and responding to me. He is the *only* one in our lives who knows exactly what's going on at all times. He knows what's been, what is, and what's coming. He knows who hurt us, why "it" (whatever "it" is for you) happened, and how to get us out of the hard spot. His word is like concrete when we need something firm to stand on, or like an elevator that we step into so that it can bring us higher. When He speaks, it changes things.

1. Write down an area of your life where you might need God to "heal" or mend something for you. It could be physical, relational, etc.

_____

2. Next, you ask God to speak a "word" about the healing or mending you need. Write down what He says. (You might remember a verse or hear a new one to look up. You might hear words that come like a whisper to your heart, remember a phrase from a show, recall song lyrics, etc.) Get God's word/heart on the matter for the healing that you need. Write down what He says.

_____

3. What does Isaiah 55:11 mean to you about what God says?

4. Next, I'd like you to pray and agree about something God is saying to you. I think it's important to "add our faith" to what He speaks. Spiritually speaking, faith is a huge factor in how we inherit and receive what God wants to do in our lives. When He reveals something specific or releases a promise over a situation, I write it down, speak it out, or I pray in agreement and thank God for His help in this situation. It's how we can partner in faith about what God is saying and it's how hooray happens for us.

ACTIVATE

Hebrews 11 is a great "faith" chapter and in every case, an action is required after God speaks. Read over Hebrews 11 and see if there is an action required about something God is saying to you.

He answers us when we call, He sends forth His word and brings healing. He has things to say about all that is happening in your life.

MEDITATION

"Your word is a lamp for me feet, a light on my path." Psalm 119:105

DAY NINETEEN

Listen

It's sure beautiful when we are hearing from God and all is going smoothly, but there are certainly times when we struggle. We struggle to hear and have faith about what God's saying, we struggle to be of any help to others. We can misinterpret God's voice, we can get excited and "add" something extra to His words, we can change the script because we don't want to hear or deliver a disappointing word, and there are about twenty other ways in which things can go sideways and a *Lost in Translation* moment can happen. In fact, *Lost in Translation* moments can happen all of the time. They happen with our friends, spouses, God, and really just about any relationship that we have. There will just come a point when someone says one thing and we hear something different, or maybe we are the ones saying one thing and someone else hears and interprets something else.

It's like using our "maps" app to get us someplace but instead of putting in "street" we punched in "lane," (because what's the difference?), and then we ended up in a completely different location. In case you're wondering, that has for sure happened to me more than I'd like to admit. We don't all speak the same language on certain topics regarding faith, family, politics, and a hundred other things.

Let's go easy on ourselves and on each other. We don't know how everyone filters things, we don't even always know how we are filtering something. We want to do our best to hear from God, get his good perspective in our lives, be good cheerleaders for others, and extend what we can. Most of the time, that will go right but when it doesn't, adjust and get a new perspective.

I tend to think that if I can just "explain myself or explain my side" of things, that everything will get straightened out. The problem with that approach is that it's really selfish, the perspective is only about me. I am only thinking about "me." If they could just understand "me" and understand what "I" meant, or "my" viewpoint, etc. It doesn't leave a lot of room for them. What did they hear, how did they feel about that, what are they experiencing after our interaction? These are good questions to ask ourselves. This is also a really helpful approach with God. What did He think of our interaction? How is He doing on the other side of our relationship? I know it can seem like an obvious thing to do in a "things went sideways" moment, but it's our nature to think about ourselves and then self-protect or self-preserve accordingly. So, I think it's pretty important to state the obvious here, these hard moments aren't just about us. If we are going to throw confetti for people and keep hooray at the forefront, then we need to be asking ourselves questions about how we are affecting others.

A couple of great questions are, what did *you* hear me say? How did what I say affect you? We can ask those same questions with God. God, this is what I believe you said to me, and this is how it's affecting me. Please continue to confirm your word to me or show me something different.

I remember when God gave me and my husband a really personal promise. It was confirmed through prayer, other people telling us they had a word, and then a dream along the same lines (we felt like God was going over the top to confirm His promise to us), and yet weeks and months went by, and nothing happened. Nothing came to fruition like we thought it would. It was a "lost in translation" moment for sure. After feeling a lot of disappointment, I realized that since God doesn't get things "wrong," I must have missed what He was saying somehow. I circled back and found some clarity in His word. "In due time, at the appointed time" is what I heard next. That would have been good to ask Him to begin with, but I rushed our time together, wrote down the word He spoke, and then ran off to tell Brian what was coming for us.

Clarity, apologies, and asking others about their point of view are super helpful when things don't go as planned. I think that instead of trying to tell our side of things or trying to promote what we are feeling as the top priority, we'd do good to really listen. Really listen.

ACTIVATION

I want to activate our listening today by asking you to practice a listening technique. Sometimes we are just "out of practice" with our listening skills. Life moves fast and with our phones at our fingertips we have a lot of opportunity to be distracted. Turn on a song and really listen to it. See if God wants to say something through the lyrics. Just listen and write down what is being hi-lighted to you. What is the message or phrase that is hitting your heart?

_____

_____

DAY TWENTY

Gifts

We've been over Ephesians 4:29 (TPT), it says that we should offer "word gifts" to each other. It's worth revisiting. I'd love for us to start the day by throwing confetti at someone with a "word gift." Let's continue to practice hearing for someone and then extend the gift of "hooray" by something you say. Take a minute and write down the name of someone in your family who could use some extra encouragement today. If you don't know, see what God says. Next, quiet your mind and ask God to give you His mind about your person. Write down a couple things you hear God say. Then send a text to your family member, something easy like, "I just wanted to encourage you today. I was praying on your behalf, and I had the sense that… (I.E. God might want to get your hopes up, so I'll be praying that hope lands with you today in all kinds of ways and that any disappointment will start to dissipate in this season, etc.)" That is just an example. You can say anything you want of course.

1. What did you hear God say? If you're having your own *Lost in Translation Moment* with God, like "What is He saying?" Or "What does He mean?" Then please circle back. Go back and ask Him again. We have to start to practice the things we are learning, otherwise we will just be people with knowledge. We want to add action and power to what we know, that's the gasoline, otherwise, the car doesn't move.

Just to note: If you're having a hard time hearing from God, then get into the word. The word of God is "alive and active" and always speaking. Read some Psalms, read through a gospel, just open up your Bible and see where it takes you.

2. I just want to acknowledge that missing it and getting things wrong is part of how we learn and then get things right. We don't hear from God perfectly; it's why we need to practice. I've never loved learning through hindsight, but it's been one of my best teachers. I correct myself, I become more gracious, and I've become gentler with myself about failure because I know it's leading me toward the answer. There is a great story in 1 Samuel 1:1-18 about a priest who mis-translates. Take a read and write down what stands out to you. Sometimes it's just nice to know that plenty of others get

tripped up and get *Lost in Translation* somehow too. The way back is really the same for all of us; review what happened, acknowledge what we need to, apologize, and pray.

PRAYER

I'd like for us to sit quietly for a couple of minutes. Let's ask the Lord to soften our hearts towards anyone who has misunderstood us (per the 1 Samuel 1 read with Hannah and Eli). Hannah's heart is admirable and incredible. I think the only way to have that kind of purity is to let go of the offenses we take up. We don't need to rehearse the wrongdoings of others toward us, or meditate on the things we've done wrong, we have a better invitation. We can sit quietly before the Lord daily and give Him the things/people that hurt us or misunderstand us. We forgive others and we forgive ourselves in order that we too are forgiven. (Forgiveness is not saying, "It's fine what you did." It just means we don't have to be the judge, we let go of the outcome. He will act on our behalf accordingly, and we can keep our hearts free from bitterness, resentment, hostility, etc.) So, close your eyes and let go of all you need to today.

ACTIVATE

If something or someone has come up in your time with God, I think it's helpful to take communion over the issue and thank God for taking up every accusation, problem, worry, and so on, on your behalf. It does us good to remember and receive what He has done on our behalf and what He's done for others. You can take communion with anything you have on hand. Start by acknowledging Him and His work on the cross as you pray; see where it takes you.

DAY TWENTY-ONE

It's Different

Today we're going to tackle yet another reason confetti throwing can be difficult for us. Sometimes, it's a *Lost in Translation* ordeal, sometimes it's our boo that gets the better of us, at times we choose not to shine, but sometimes instead of extending we are shrinking. This chapter picks on page 100 in the book (just for reference) and it deals with some of the reasons why not staying our size is a problem for us.

We are going to all have a different expression of how we extend confetti to people. We have different strengths, talents, and interpretations of things, that is the beauty of uniqueness. Uniqueness can feel like a hindrance if you start comparing your "portion" (what you get from the Lord/who you are, etc.) with others. For instance, if the good gifting or uniqueness in others causes you to start shrinking, you might have a smallness problem. Staying small will hold you back from what you have to offer and how you choose to extend, so it's important we explore this together.

Let's first take a look at the story in Numbers 13. I'll run through it quickly. The Israelites were about to take their promised land (never easy) that God had waiting for them, so they went to spy it out and give a report to their leader about how good it looked etc. They ran into a couple of problems because any time we are going to take "new land" that God wants to give us, there is always a testing or contending before our entrance. Please read through Numbers 13.

    1. What were a couple of things that caused the Israelites to shrink?

_____

_____

Sometimes, too many opinions can be a real problem for us. When we weigh things by what other people are saying or what we're seeing, instead of by what God has spoken to us, there is always going to be a discrepancy. We will have to make a daily choice to believe God over our circumstances, our feelings, what culture says, or how things "appear." For us to stand on His promises and hold onto the words He speaks to us and over us, we have to know what He's actually saying.

2. What "new land" (promises or promised places) do you want to take this season? I.E. what are you believing God for, or need Him to do for you?

_____

_____

3. What is God saying about that specific situation for you? (If you don't know, take some time to ask Him.)

_____

_____

4. When I'm believing God for "new land," (for something He's promised or a new direction) I need to rehearse His answers to myself, an affirmation of sorts. It creates expectation in me, it pushes out the lies, helps me stay my size, changes my perspective, and builds courage for me to tackle the hard thing in front of me. Write down (again) a "mantra/affirmation, something you can repeat when you feel yourself starting to shrink or feel small.

_____

_____

I just wrote one down for my daughter the other day. She was struggling through some approval stuff, and we needed to get her back into alignment with truth. It went something like this: "I am made exactly the way God planned. I am unique and wonderful. I'm a good friend and I have a lot to offer others. I am not alone and never will be. When I am myself, I am blessed, known, and seen. When I am myself, others will be drawn to me. I have good ideas. I am smart, fun, talented, and creative."

You get it, she needed a new lens and a greater truth to rehearse for a couple of weeks after she had been feeling low. Our mantras/affirmations change in different seasons, but they should always point us back to what God has to say about the subject matter that we are dealing with. The words should affect positive change in us and re-align us with a truer reality. It's like getting a spiritual chiropractic adjustment and honestly, who doesn't need that from time to time?

Write down your words here.

_____

_____

_____

_____

_____

ACTIVATE

Let's keep the confetti falling for yourself. Maybe you need to text a friend and ask them to give you a word of encouragement. Maybe you want to get silent and invite God to speak. You might want to ask your husband to pray a blessing over you. You could head to a bookstore and stand in front of the magazine rack and see what phrases pop out at you. However you need to get a good word for yourself, I invite you to do it. Heaven has confetti to throw your way, ask for it.

DAY TWENTY-TWO

Inward

Warn your friends and family they're about to be drowning in confetti. This week we are going to look at a couple of Bible passages that will help us extend what we have to others, not just practically, but also from a place internally. Any of us could take action steps that will get the confetti-throwing job done, but we are after lasting change. A change that will keep our hands clapping and throwing confetti long after this study is over. For that, we need to look inward.

We're going to read Colossians 3. The whole book is transformative so if you have the time, it's worth your while to start in chapter one, but today let's go to Col. 3:1-11

1. Make note of anything that specifically stands out to you.

_____

_____

2. Throwing confetti requires a heavenly perspective and we can get that lens when we "set our minds on things above." It moves us from an internal and natural view, to a more heavenly one, and things look a lot different from "on high." What's one situation or person you need to get a "things above" perspective on and how do you want to practically do that?

_____

_____

3. We can talk ourselves out of throwing confetti for people pretty easily, that's why getting God's perspective is so important to our hooray lifestyle. Renewing our minds and changing our focus really does affect how we act and participate with others. Memorizing scripture and reading the word are an important practice in our daily lives with a "things above approach" to life.

Write down one scripture from this chapter in Colossians and read over it daily this week.

_____

_____

ACTIVATE

Write down the same verse you just wrote for yourself on a note card and then pray about who needs this word of encouragement. You can write their name on a card and pray it over them, or you can give it to them this week.

DAY TWENTY-THREE

put it away

Paul says that there are things we have to "die to" and things we have to "put away." Our flesh is always fighting to narrate our life, the problem is that our flesh is not in accordance with a "things above" approach. I think this is where confetti can get really held up because our flesh is only thinking about how to appease and gratify "self." If we don't die to some things and put some things away, then renewal will take a whole lot longer for us. Please reflect.

1. Is there anything in your life that you need to "put to death" as Paul says? (Col. 3:5) After you write it down, then please genuinely pray for the Holy Spirit to help you in this process. It is not easy without Gods help to close a chapter in our life.

   _____

   _____

2. I think it's difficult to just end something without replacing it with a new practice. For instance, if your struggle is gossip, it's good to replace that current problem with a new action. Before you say something, picture that person standing next to Jesus with His arm around them. Then actively say one or two truthful/encouraging things about the person you want to speak poorly about. Replacing your current action with a more "renewed" approach will be helpful. Write down one action item you can start to practice *in place* of the thing you want to "put to death."

   _____

   _____

3. Paul mentions idolatry in his list of "putting things to death." An idol is anything that would steal our affection or attention away from Jesus. It's something we use to console, comfort, give us confidence,

or strengthen ourselves that isn't Him. Tim Keller says it's "When we allow something other than God to be the center of hearts *true* happiness, contentment, meaning, purpose, or identity." Don't worry, we all have them. Identify any areas of idolatry in your life. (I.E. kids, relationships, comfort, approval, control, power, things, etc.)

_____

_____

4. In Col. 3:8, Paul tells us that there are specific things we need to "put away." Putting something away is an active choice and once we make it, we also have to choose not to "bring it back out." That list would keep any of us from throwing confetti toward others. Look at the list and write down what you need to "put away" so that your confetti isn't hindered. Of course, there are probably other things not on this list, so feel free to expand.

_____

_____

_____

CLOSING

Today felt a little heavy talking about the things that hang us up and the "old self." I just want to remind you that our journey to living fully alive, healed, and transformed is a lifelong process. At times, there will be circumstances that get in the way of our confetti, attitudes that need adjusting, and motives that need to be put back in check. If we were perfect, we wouldn't need such a kind and forgiving Savior. We wouldn't need the Holy Spirit's help, we wouldn't need the instruction to "set our minds on things above" because it would be in our nature to already do it. But we do need God's kind instruction. We need His Spirit, His graces, and His constant forgiveness. We won't have confetti ready without Him. So, go easy on yourself, we are all going to "get it" one day soon, and until then, we will work on how to have confetti ready within us.

DAY TWENTY-FOUR

Wardrobe

We are going to continue to read through Colossians today and focus on our wardrobe. What we "wear" seems to be of the utmost importance. And though I love a good shopping day and things on sale, I'm not talking about what we wear externally. This passage is about how we "clothe" ourselves internally. Please read through Colossians 3:12-17.

1. We have a heavenly wardrobe that we're to be fitted with and Paul points out that this wardrobe is for "God's chosen ones" (Col. 3:12). Write down the list of "accessories" he mentions.

   _____

   _____

2. I'm pretty thoughtful about what I'm wearing. I like when my outfit can be both cute and comfortable, but Paul's list isn't always going to feel comfortable on us. It might feel more like wearing a pair of jeans that are a couples sizes too small, you have to suck it in, and that can feel really constricting. Look and the list and write down what feels like "your size" and what feels a little harder for you to wear.

   _____

   _____

   _____

3. Humility, kindness, and forgiveness; these are all important traits in the life of a believer. Much damage can be done in relationships if we forget to put these on. These are essential to our "outfit" if we are going to throw confetti for others. So many hearts get hindered and hands stop clapping

because of unforgiveness, or a lack of kindness and humility. We need to be intentional with the things we decide to put on. Please reflect and write down what you want to start "wearing."

_____

_____

_____

ACTIVATE

Sometimes God speaks to me through clothes. It's one of my "love languages." I thought a good activation would be to buy something new for yourself. Look at Paul's list again and think about what you need to be "wearing" this season in order to better throw confetti. Maybe it's a necklace with the letter "H" on it for humility, or "C" for confetti. Maybe it's a shirt that says "love." Maybe it's a belt that reminds you to "strap these things on." Honestly, I could make just about anything fit with wardrobe symbolism. But sincerely pray, and then keep your eyes open, you might be surprised by what you find.

DAY TWENTY-FIVE

Motive

Colossians 3 is a complex scripture to get our hearts around. It's both hopeful and challenging. It's exciting to have a new way to do life, to set our minds on something higher than what we see in front of us. That old nature is real though, and vying for our attention, trying to make sure we feed our appetites. There are things we have to "put on" and things we have to "take off" and then there are the motives of our hearts. Today we are going to explore our motives.

1. What is the most challenging verse for you in this section of scripture (Col. 3) and why is that?

   _____

   _____

2. Read through Col. 3:17 and Col. 3:23 and write down the similarities from these passages.

   _____

   _____

   _____

3. I wish everyone's (including my own) motives and intentions were always pure and lovely. Unless we really do "die" to our "old man's" ways, we are going to have some really mixed motives. This passage does outline some how-to's for us. It's not a matter of "what" we need to do, but a matter of "will" we do it. If we choose to put some things into practice from this chapter, our hearts will be greatly affected. When our hearts are affected inwardly, we can't help but have a change in expression outwardly. We will start throwing confetti from a genuinely loving place with a motive that has nothing to do with us. We will do things "unto the Lord" with gratitude, not doing it for "man" but

for Him. Write down one thing from this passage that you can consciously start doing today that affects your motive. What is it and how will you incorporate it into your daily life?

_____

_____

_____

PRAYER

I want to close with a verse to pray out loud and meditate on. When I think of meditating on scripture, I think about "chewing" on the verse, like I'm chewing food. We need to "nibble on it" and see what it tastes like. Let it fill us up and then internally digest it. What we eat internally affects us externally. When we feed ourselves scripture it brings health to our whole body. Health to our hearts, minds, and motives. Read over Col.3:23 four or five times and recall it though out the day.

MEDIATION

"Whatever you do, do it from the heart, as something done for the Lord and not for people" (Col. 3:23).

DAY TWENTY-SIX

The Heart

The heart, the heart, the heart. It's central to all we do. Confetti isn't just conjured up out of nowhere, confetti comes from a place deep within. It comes from the heart and by practicing engaging our hearts. In fact, Paul tells us that "whatever" we do, we need to do it from the heart. "Whatever you do, do it from the heart, as something done for the Lord and not for people" (Col. 3:23).

1. We should probably start by addressing the heart. Take a minute and write down how your heart is doing today (do you feel connected, centered, engaged, etc. What is your emotional health feeling like?). It's hard to throw confetti when our hearts are hurting. It's not impossible but it's important we take a pulse on how our hearts are doing.

_____

_____

2. What does your heart really need this season? Does it need healing? Love? Time with friends or time in the Word? I know there's not always a quick resolution to the things our hearts need but it's important to process and let Jesus speak to that for us.

_____

_____

_____

3. This seems like an important time to pause for prayer. Back to Psalm 139, which enlists God to search our hearts. "Search me, oh God, and know my heart." I love this verse. Our hearts can be difficult to assess, sometimes we need God to speak to us or reveal something that we don't know or can't see. Our hearts could still be in distress over something, weighed down by worry, unhealed, uncertain, hard, or angry. They could also be expectant, hopeful, happy. Whatever the condition,

God sees and knows at all times, and I think it's important to allow God to address us daily over matters of our hearts. Read through Psalm 139 and then sit quietly and see what surfaces in your time or throughout the rest of the day. Write down anything that gets revealed to you.

_____

_____

_____

_____

_____

CLOSING

I think it would do our hearts some good to address the needs of another. It can be good practice after we look internally to redirect our focus externally. Colossians 3:17 is one of my favorite confetti verses. It reads, "and whatever you do, in word or deed…" It implies that WE WILL do things. We will do things with our words and with our deeds. We will do, no matter how we are currently feeling. This is how heavenly confetti gets thrown. We align our hearts with a pure motive, open ourselves up to what God wants to do and how He wants to use us. We use our words and our "deeds" to be hooray for others because God has so generously been hooray for us. I'm sure you know all that by now, but just in case, I thought I'd make a note of it.

Why don't we close today by throwing confetti for someone new? I don't care how you do it, use your words or your deeds and confetti someone. Maybe a stranger, maybe someone in the grocery line, maybe buy a drink for the car behind you at the coffee drive thru. How you choose to confetti is up to you. Think about your motive, ask God what He has in mind, and then match your words or your deeds to encourage someone today.

DAY TWENTY-SEVEN

How He Does It

Today we're going to focus on what it looks like when Jesus throws confetti. How does Jesus go about hooray and what effect does it have on others? Of course, I can't fit it all into a couple of days. His life transformed and eternally changed so many who walked closely with Him and even those who only briefly interacted with Him. The opportunities we have to affect people and offer hope are truly endless.

Please read through Luke 18:35-43 and note any observations you make about how the blind man postures himself to be confettied by Jesus.

1. Jesus has confetti in His pockets at all times for people; it gets unlocked differently depending on the circumstances. Sometimes, it looks like healing and is hope extended. Sometimes, it looks like Jesus speaking truth by a word of encouragement or correction. In this specific case, Jesus asks the man a question, the same question I believe He still asks to us today. What does Jesus ask the man (Luke 13:41)?

   _____

   _____

2. Sometimes, it takes Jesus a long time to do something "instantly" (Luke 13:43). Who knows how long the blind man sat waiting to be looked upon, waiting for confetti? Do you have a personal need that needs attention from Heaven? Is there something you want to "see," or something you've been waiting for? Don't hesitate to write it down. Call out to Him as the blind man did and see how Jesus responds to you.

   _____

   _____

3. In Luke 18:37 my ESV translation reads, "Jesus was passing by. So, the man cried out to Him…"

The man saw opportunity and didn't hesitate. His poor condition didn't keep him from God, it's what caused him to cry out. He couldn't heal himself or no doubt he would have. I wonder if that has any correlation to anything in our lives. Don't hesitate about the things you want/need. Look up some of these verses and write down what they instruct us to do:

a. **1 Kings 3:5**

b. **James 4:2**

c. **Mathew 21:22**

d. **John 16:24**

PRAYER

Jesus gave each of us a mandate when it comes to *how* we can throw confetti for others and be a voice of hooray. It doesn't have anything to do with our gifts or positioning in life, so no one gets a pass. Throwing confetti for others opens people up to a greater truth. This is the hope, the message, the megaphone Jesus has put in our hands, and He has graciously given us a helper to do it. The Holy Spirit guides and leads us so that we don't have to guess about where to go and what to do.

Jesus speaks about our commissioning in Mathew 28:18, Luke 24:46-49, and again in Acts 1:8. Of course, how we fulfill that mission will look different for each of us. It will have our own flavor, and we will go about it in different ways. Sit with these verses for a little bit. Look them up, write down what stands out, and then prayerfully consider what your part is in all of this.

DAY TWENTY-EIGHT

Pieces

These next couple of days we are going to focus on your specific piece, the part that you are gifted to play in throwing confetti for others. How are you uniquely wired to encourage and celebrate the people God has you next to? Let's start by answering a couple of questions.

1. What brings you joy and excitement when it comes to how you serve others? Do you like to host people and have them over? Do you like to cook/bake/paint/give gifts/write cards/make people feel welcome/help them practically/clean/run errands/etc.? These are just some ideas to get you thinking about how you personally like to be a blessing to other people.

_____

_____

_____

2. How do you like to "be hooray" to others? What do you have to offer? What kind of time during the day? What talents or resources do you have available to you? (By the way, the only "ability" we need for God to use us is "availability." That's not mine, I heard a speaker say that once and I'm holding onto it.) How do you like to express your love/encouragement/support to people? What age groups or demographics of people do you like to be around? Make some notes about how you'd like to start to throw confetti for people.

_____

_____

_____

3. In the Bible, Paul talks about "spiritual gifts" that each of us have. I think there are many gifts but there are some he lists specifically. These are gifts that help us throw confetti uniquely and accomplish the work Jesus has called us to do. They are listed in 1 Corinthians 12-14, Romans 12, and Ephesians 4. Do you know what some of your "spiritual gifts" are? If this concept is new to you or you'd just like a refresher, there are good quizzes online (spiritual gift assessment tests) to take that can help point to some of them for you.

ACTIVATE

Sit in prayer for a couple of minutes. Ask the Holy Spirit to reveal to you an area of your gifting. Ask Him to speak one word about a gift you have, then write down one way you can use your "gift" to bless to someone. What is "the gift" and how will you extend yourself today?

DAY TWENTY-NINE

Practices

You are almost finished! Hopefully, by now you are neck deep in confetti throwing, surrounded by so much sparkle you can barely see straight. Truly, the goal was to come out of things that keep us from cheering for others and to keep our hands clapping. People need what you have and sometimes, we need real reminders to keep that truth in front of us. What you have to give is important, nobody else can give it but you. You won't know what the cost is to others if you hold back what you have to offer the world, but I can tell you that others will be greatly affected. Your expression of love is needed today, in this time in history, with the people God has placed you beside. So, please throw the confetti.

1. After assessing your "part" from last week and the ways you like to throw confetti for others, what is one thing you realized about yourself and how God has wired you?

_____

_____

2. Read through Romans 12: 1-7. I want to make sure that our pockets are padded with confetti, and as this verse suggests, there are a couple of ways to go about doing that. What verses grabbed you today from Romans 12 and why is that? What you have is for others and what they have is for you. It's why our offering to others is so important, because "we belong to each other" (Eph. 4:25b TPT). God has given you something that is for the people around you, please don't hold back what is uniquely yours to give.

_____

_____

3. When we think about our own bodies, we know we need all of our different parts to function in the way that was designed for them. We need to move our body and treat it well to keep it functioning properly. The "part" we have to play is instrumental in the whole body of Christ, and we want our

part to be fully operational. After reading through the verses in Romans, are you motivated to play your part in the body? Do you feel equipped to do so? Why or why not? Take some time to think and journal through this. It's an important next step in your confetti throwing. Something may be keeping you hindered. It could be fear of stepping out, not feeling equipped, rejection, etc. Write it down here.

_____

_____

_____

Lastly, I just want to stand on my soapbox for a quick second and speak to you straight. So here it is, confetti throwing comes in many forms. It can be fun, messy, personal, or impersonal, anointed, or random. We will all throw it differently and it will always land differently. We don't need to worry about the outcome, we just need to step into opportunities as God gives them to us.

Let's be prayerful and consider how we can use all of the "pieces" (time, gifts, talents, resources, etc.) that are ours and then take steps to actively love, bless, and honor others. I want to remind you that you have a sacred part to play in this world. Don't get complacent when it comes to your serving others. Don't allow needless competing or comparing to hold back what you have to offer. Deal with the hurt that's happened in your life. Move past self-protection and self-absorption and see who you can bless, because confetti won't fall if we don't play our part.

MEDITATION

Romans 12:10 has something for us to consider. Please look up and write down Romans 12:10. Then consider what you might need to shift or incorporate today in order to show love and honor in a tangible way?

_____

ACTIVATE

Today, I am going to ask you to throw confetti in a way that might feel a little uncomfortable, like when my son has to dribble a ball with his left hand. It's not completely complicated but it doesn't feel natural. What is one way you can go out of your way to practically show your love "large, patient, and gentle?" (Ok, two out of three isn't bad.) Throw confetti today for someone while engaging your heart in deep love. Touch base with a mother or father-in-law. Grab some groceries for a neighbor. I won't tell you how to do it but think intentionally about it for a minute and see what surfaces in your heart. Write it here:

_____

_____

_____

_____

_____

DAY THIRTY

Let It Fall

Today we are going to practice hooray. I know, a real shocker, right? I want you to do it with words. First, let's center ourselves on some scripture and remember why this is so good for our hearts to practice. "Let every activity of your lives and every word that comes from your lips be drenched with the beauty of our Lord Jesus, the Anointed One…" Col.3:17 TPT). This verse is quite literally life changing when it comes to our offering, I had to end with it.

1. Today we are going to drench our words in beauty. We are going to issue hooray by extending an encouraging word. We are going to practice pulling heaven down for a heart that needs to hear something good. Pray for someone and write it down in a note, something you believe God is saying over them. Make sure your words match God's heart for them. Simply start by asking for the Holy Spirit to give you a picture of something that could really bless them. This isn't a time for us to offer advice. Empty your mind of your own opinions and let God speak and use you as the mailman today to deliver some good news. So, who are you going to "deliver" it to and what is the message?

_____

_____

_____

2. It occurred to me as I typed Colossians three (Let every word be drenched in beauty) that there might be some "not so beautiful words" we need to deal with. Words we've spoken over others or words we remember that someone has spoken over or about us. For instance, I ran into a friend the other day and though we've parted ways for this season, I have so much love for her. I went right over to her as soon as I saw her. We talked and caught up, it was special and sweet. But as I walked away, I started to remember all of the things that she poorly and inaccurately spoke about me to others. The ugly stuff got back to me, and I started feeling hurt all over again. I had to make a choice to not think about those things and instead, remind myself I have confetti for her. I closed my eyes for a quick second and I asked the Lord to say something to me. His response was simple, "love does." Love forgives, love doesn't hold onto grudges. Love blesses, honors, protects, and perseveres.

So, I started to pray for her and bless her future. I asked for continual healing over anything in our past and gave my hurt to God. This was how I confettied her. She wouldn't have seen it, but I know it was falling for her.

Take a minute and see if there's any "clean-up" you might need to do in regard to hurtful words. See how the Lord might ask you to pray for someone or confess and repent for anything you've spoken lately that might cause harm to another heart. Then think about how your words can be drenched in beauty and then given to those around you. I love that word picture from Colossians, what a thought.

_____

_____

3. We are going to stay on the theme of words. I have a couple more verses I want us to look up and think about. Please read them and write down what our words can do.

   A. **Proverbs 10:21**

   _____

   B. **Proverbs 10:31**

   _____

   C. **Proverbs 12:18**

   _____

   D. **Mathew 12:36**

   _____

4. In Job 22:28 (KJV), it says that "what we decree will take place." When we "decree" something, it's like we are commanding that thing to happen. We are enforcing an edict of legal authority on it by what we are saying. As God's children, He has given us authority in the spiritual realm, that allows

us to shift things by what we say. By faith, we can decree something and believe for God's intention to come to pass in our lives and the lives of others. Take a couple of minutes and "activate this word." Write down or say aloud some decrees over your family. These can be promises you pray out loud and ask God to establish them for you. You can speak divine healing or blessed outcomes about something that's happening. Start decreeing blessings over your circumstances or future and believe for God to act on your behalf.

_____

_____

_____

_____

CLOSING

I want to close up our time and have you read over Psalm 23. Remind yourself of God's care for you, let confetti come for *you*. He is crazy about you. He loves you, leads you, sees you, anoints you, and has good things He has prepared to give you. Take some time to get quiet and ask the Holy Spirit how He would like to throw confetti for you today? Don't second-guess yourself. Maybe He has something He wants you to buy, maybe it's rest He wants to give you with a nap or a bath. Maybe it's a coffee date with a friend or lunch with a spouse. Listen, write it down, and then just do what He says. Confetti only falls when we take action. How will confetti come for you today?

Lastly, I just want to say WELL DONE! I want confetti to fall from the sky and land in your lap. I want your jaw to drop in awe. I want you to feel seen by God today. I am praying that something so uniquely special happens to you today/tonight/this week, that you would know that you know that you know, it was God himself issuing confetti on your behalf.

I hear this in my spirit for you; "The Lord bless you, and keep you (protect, sustain, and guard you), The Lord make His face shine upon you (with favor), and be gracious to you (surrounding you with loving kindness), The Lord lift up His face upon you (with divine approval), And give you peace" (Num. 6:24-26 AMP).

I pray you hear His voice more loudly and with greater ease, clarity, and accuracy than you have in the past. I pray for you to sense the Holy Spirit's applause over your life and over your new practices. I am tearing up as I write this just thinking of how Heaven might want to gift you with something special. May you receive texts of appreciation, letters in the mail, a word of encouragement, or find something you wanted for yourself "on-sale" and so on and so on and so on. May confetti keep falling until you're buried in it.

I pray for the deeper things too. That relationships will be reconciled, that your heart and the hearts around you will be continually transformed. I pray your mantras, prayers, declarations, and decrees will be established and fulfilled. I pray your faith will rise, and you will come into a deeper knowing of who you are, how you are made, and the One who cares so greatly for you. I pray you know how much your applause means to those around you, and that you will regularly offer confetti. And I sincerely hope that you yourself will be continually confettied in this life.

> Throwing confetti is a continual practice and something we want to stay good at, don't hesitate to pick up this study in another season. Bless you, and happy confetti throwing!
>
> **DEANN CARPENTER**

ABOUT THE AUTHOR

DeAnn Carpenter writes, teaches, and serves because she's passionate about supporting and celebrating others. Together she and her husband, Brian Carpenter, founded and direct the nonprofit, Refuge Foundation. (See https://Refuge.Rest) They reside in Montana with their two kids, Asher and Ruby. There they train and develop staff to care for, serve, and support leaders.

Refuge is currently in multiple locations in the American West, bringing reprieve and rest to leaders from all over the world. DeAnn helps with staff development and directs the Refuge W.I.L.D experience (see http://RefugeWild.org), which guides women in rest, deeper living in God, and one another.

DeAnn grew up in the Great Plains of North Dakota before moving to Montana. In Montana she attended the Yellowstone Valley Bible Institute, where she worked on staff serving youth, young adults, and women's ministries. She had flipped many houses, worked in the salon industry, taught at women's conferences, and will always be "in the business of transformation." She has a love for good coffee, great Thai food, and hanging with her friends and family. You can reach out to her on her website at www.deanncarpenter.com

NOTES

NOTES

NOTES

NOTES

NOTES

NOTES

NOTES